DB2 11:
The Ultimate Database for Cloud, Analytics, and Mobile

John Campbell

Chris Crone

Gareth Jones

Surekha Parekh

Jay Yothers

MC Press Online, LLC

Boise, ID 83703 USA

DB2 11: The Ultimate Database for Cloud, Analytics, and Mobile

John Campbell, Chris Crone, Gareth Jones, Surekha Parekh, and Jay Yothers

First Edition
First Printing—October 2014

MC Press Online, LLC
Corporate Offices: 3695 W. Quail Heights Court, Boise, ID 83703-3861 USA
Sales and Customer Service: (208) 629-7275 ext. 500; service@mcpressonline.com
Permissions and Bulk/Special Orders: mcbooks@mcpressonline.com
www.mcpressonline.com • www.mc-store.com

ISBN: 978-1-58347-401-3   WB201409

About the Authors

John Campbell (*campbelj@uk.ibm.com*) is an IBM Distinguished Engineer reporting to the Director for z/OS Development at the IBM Silicon Valley Lab. He has extensive experience of DB2 in terms of systems, database, and applications design. John specializes in design for high performance and data sharing. He is one of IBM's foremost authorities for implementing high-end database/transaction-processing applications.

"I strongly encourage any customer planning a migration to DB2 11, or even already executing a project to migrate to DB2 11, to read this book, as it will help the respective installation migrate faster and safely to the new release."

Chris Crone (*cjc@us.ibm.com*) is a Distinguished Engineer with the IBM DB2 for z/OS Development team, where he has worked for 25 years. He is the team lead for the RDS Execution Engine team and has contributed to many SQL-related items while working on more 10 releases of DB2. More recently, Chris has been working on improving the performance and scalability of DB2 for z/OS.

"DB2 11 has added major new capability in the form of application compatibility with DB2 10. This support will enable customers to confidently migrate their systems to DB2 11, while ensuring that their applications will continue to behave as they did in DB2 10 without change. I hope you will read this book and understand how you can unlock this new capability."

Gareth Jones (*jonesgth@uk.ibm.com*) has been in IT since 1985, when he worked in the United Kingdom for an IBM customer. His first real contact with DB2 was when, as an IMS Systems Programmer and DBA, he was handed the job of migrating DB2 from V1.3 to V2.1, and he hasn't looked back since. He spent eight years as a contractor, gaining experience in France, the Netherlands, and the UK, before joining IBM as a permanent employee in 2000. Gareth worked for several years in IBM's Strategic Outsourcing division, and in BetaWorks, before joining the DB2 for z/OS SWAT Team under the leadership of John Campbell, taking advantage of the opportunity to work with many customers around the world.

"This book is a valuable source of information for customers planning to migrate to DB2 11, for those who are already in the process of migrating, and for those who are planning to exploit some of the new features. It will help you to achieve your objectives safely and successfully."

Surekha Parekh (*surekhaparekh@uk.ibm.com*) is IBM's World-Wide Marketing Program Director. She has more than 25 years' experience in B2B Market Management across a broad range of IT products and solutions with proven results. Surekha currently leads the Marketing for DB2 for z/OS globally and is responsible for market strategy, planning, and execution of tactics in IBM. A successful campaign and brand manager, Surekha has led several IBM global campaigns, including the 30th Anniversary of DB2. She is particularity customer-focused and understands the importance of Customer Relationship Management.

Surekha also leads the Social Media Strategy for Information Management on System z. In this role, she has built several loyal social media communities for IBM on LinkedIn, Twitter, Google+, and Facebook, with over 10,000 members. Surekha also developed "The World of DB2" community (*www.worldofdb2.com*), a dedicated DB2 online community with over 3,000 members.

Based in Warwick, United Kingdom, Surekha is a passionate marketer and a member of Chartered Marketers. She represents IBM on the International DB2 User Group (IDUG) committee and is currently the IDUG Marketing Chair.

"We hope you enjoy this book, and we hope it saves you time and money. Find out why DB2 11 is still the #1 Enterprise Data Server and the choice for most Fortune 100® companies."

Jay Yothers (*yothers@us.ibm.com*) is an IBM DB2 for z/OS architect. He has been part of the DB2 Development organization since the very first release of DB2 and has designed and developed many key features of DB2 for z/OS. He has been awarded more than 20 patents for his work in DB2 for z/OS. Jay is a frequent speaker at conferences such as IDUG, SHARE, and Insight and at seminars, webcasts, user group meetings, and executive briefings, bringing a wealth of knowledge and experience to such events.

"I recommend this book to customers interested in improving the performance and functional capability of their database system. It describes the performance advantages and additional functional capability of V11 along with its simplified and relatively easier migration process."

Contents

Case Studies

Introduction

by Surekha Parekh

In the current economic climate, businesses are under significant pressure to control costs and increase efficiency to improve their bottom line. IBM® DB2® for z/OS® customers around the world are still trying to gain competitive advantage by doing more with less: more business insight, more performance, more operational efficiency, more functionality, and more productivity with less cost, quicker time to market, and a lower TCO.

DB2 11 helps customers address key business issues by delivering innovations and business benefits in the following important areas:

- **Even more out-of-the-box CPU savings:**

  o Up to 10% for complex OLTP

  o Up to 10% for update-intensive batch

  o Up to 40% for queries

  o Up to 25% for uncompressed tables and 40% for compressed tables

- **Enhanced resiliency**

  o Fewer planned outages, fewer REORGs, faster recovery

  o Cost-effective archiving, ability to access warm/cold data in a single query

- **Business-critical analytics**

  o DB2 Analytics Accelerator performance enhancements

  o Big data integration

  o In-transaction realtime scoring

  o Advanced QMF™ analytic capabilities with mobile support

- **Simpler, faster upgrades for faster ROI**

  o 16X faster catalog migration

  o Protection from incompatible changes

  o Repeatable testing with real workloads and integrated cloning

We have seen many top 10 lists around DB2 11; in this section, we summarize the top 10 reasons why we feel it is the right time for customers to upgrade to DB2 11. We all know that *support for DB2 Version 10 will be withdrawn from Marketing* on July 6, 2015. However, there are many more reasons to migrate; users will see significant benefits from DB2 11.

Top 10 Reasons to Upgrade to DB2 11 for z/OS

1. Reduced COSTS! Even more cost savings—up to 40%

2. Business analytics for realtime decision making made simple

3. Enabled for big data and cloud phenomenon!

4. Enabled for a mobile world—with world-class JSON datastore

5. SPEED! Simpler, faster migration for FASTER ROI

6. TRUST—ENHANCED RESILIENCY 24x7

7. UNMATCHED DATA SECURITY in the industry

8. Certified for SAP applications from day 1—first time in history

9. Industry-leading Optimizer gets even better!

10. Improved productivity with DB2 11

1. Reduced Costs: Even More Cost Savings—Up to 40%

DB2 11 helps your bottom line with out-of-the-box CPU savings for online transaction processing (OLTP), batch, and query workloads to help you get the most out of your investment. These savings range up to 40 percent, depending on the workload. Additional savings and performance improvements may be found by leveraging DB2 features and making application changes.

Transparent archive capabilities help keep more data available with improved performance and reduced storage costs.

Specialty engines continue to add value for many IBM clients. DB2 11 delivers additional processing that is directed to execute under enclave SRBs and authorized to execute on a zIIP specialty engine, which can provide additional cost savings and efficiencies in your System z® environment.

2. Business Analytics for Realtime Decision Making Made Simple

Business analytics is now business-critical. DB2 11 makes it easier to bring analytic components closer to the core operational data—reducing latency, complexity, and costs while improving data quality and governance. Improved query, lightning-fast analytics, and reporting facilities will help you outperform your competitors, reduce risks, and aid confident decision making with "Real-Time Data."

3. Enabled for Big Data and Cloud Phenomenon

Few IT professionals can have missed the big data and cloud phenomenon that has manifested itself in recent years. Despite the undeniable value of the highly structured operational data held within enterprise applications, a vast amount of less-structured data is being generated by social media streams, telemetry, click streams, and many other sources. Being able to analyze these big data sources undoubtedly holds significant value for many organizations, but the sheer volume and velocity at which the data is produced makes it a very challenging task for traditional database systems.

In response to this, a number of tools and techniques have emerged centered on the open source Hadoop framework, including IBM's InfoSphere® BigInsights™ technology. While these technologies address many of the challenges inherent in the analysis of big data, they also introduce new ones for organizations wanting to gain new insights by integrating the analysis of big data with core operational information. DB2 11 delivers some highly significant new features to allow DB2 and Hadoop/BigInsights to work together and better leverage each platform's respective strengths. This capability allows data to flow in both directions between DB2 and BigInsights, and from BigInsights to DB2.

The new integration capabilities delivered within DB2 11 allow organizations to more easily and efficiently combine the results of big data analysis with up-to-date operational data from DB2 OLTP databases, significantly increasing the practical value of any insights obtained.

4. Enabled for a Mobile World
—With a World-Class JSON Datastore

With the enormous growth of smart phones and applications, customers everywhere are building systems of engagement using mobile technology. These new systems are extremely agile and typically use JavaScript® and JSON. Application developers are pushing for JSON datastores that they see in the NoSQL world, and DB2 11 is evolving to be a world-class JSON datastore, so you don't need to leave DB2 to get these benefits.

5. Speed: Faster Migration for Faster ROI

The faster an upgrade can be completed, the faster you can see the return on investment. DB2 11 catalog upgrades are up to 16 times faster than in DB2 10. Additional access path stability improvements help maintain and even improve performance when upgrading to DB2 11, providing more stability from day 1.

DB2 11 for z/OS introduces the concept of *application compatibility*, which enables you to separate release upgrades from application changes that may be needed to take advantage of a new function. New tracing capabilities help identify applications that may need changes, and then you can make plans for those application changes independent of upgrade schedules and plans. When the new DB2 version has been upgraded, the application will run as if it were on the previous DB2 version. Application changes can now be scheduled within the application's own development cycle. As the changes are completed, the application can then take advantage of the new capabilities in the new DB2 release. Separating application changes from database upgrades greatly simplifies planning and also speeds the upgrade itself.

Optim™ Workload Replay (OWR) lets you capture, save your production workloads, and then replay them in test environments to reduce migration risk. You can identify problems earlier using validation reports and performance tuning, avoid production outages, and increase production stability. OWR is integrated with the DB2 Cloning Tool to cost-effectively and easily copy your production database to your test environment. This single, repeatable process can dramatically reduce migration test efforts and investments while improving results.

6. Trust: Enhanced Resiliency 24x7

In DB2 11, the legendary resiliency of DB2 has been increased even further. Real-world proven resiliency and security are some of the core reasons why clients choose DB2 and System z. DB2 11 continues to raise the bar with additional capabilities for even higher availability and resiliency. Online schema enhancements allow changes to database objects while maximizing availability of the changed objects. The number of REORG jobs needed has been reduced while, at the same time, delivering performance improvements of up to 20 percent. Additional performance improvements of up to 70 percent for LOAD and up to 40 percent for RECOVER drive additional benefits and resiliency.

7. Unmatched Data Security in the Industry

Data security means protecting a database from destructive forces and the unwanted actions of unauthorized users. DB2 for z/OS remains the market leader when it comes to protecting your mission-critical data. "Bet your business" security has been extended to simplify management and compliance.

DB2 received a comprehensive overhaul of its security features within the DB2 10 for z/OS release. DB2 11 adds some important new functionality, including RACF® exit enhancements and column masking.

8. Certified for SAP Applications from Day 1—First Time in History

DB2 11 has been certified for SAP applications at General Availability (GA). This is the first time in the history of DB2 and the first time for any new release of any database supported by SAP. The day 1 certification of DB2 11 demonstrates the close technical SAP/DB2 collaboration and great stability of the DB2 11 product and enables SAP clients to immediately take advantage of the numerous DB2 11 enhancements. DB2 11 SAP certification not only addresses the latest SAP NetWeaver release, but all SAP NetWeaver releases as of 7.00 will be certified for DB2 11. For details, please visit the SAP DB2 for z/OS Community (*http://scn.sap.com/community/db2-for-z-os*).

9. Industry-Leading Optimizer Gets Even Better

No new release would be complete without further enhancements to DB2's industry-leading Optimizer—the key component that allows it to pick the most efficient access path for a given query.

The major items delivered as part of DB2 11 include:

- Hash join/sparse index enhancements
- Predicate indexability improvements
- Duplicate removal
- DPSIs and page range screening
- Optimizer RUNSTATS feedback
- Extended optimization

10. Improved Productivity with DB2 11

DB2 11 continues to build on the best practices of previous releases, providing many enhanced features—such as transparent archiving, XQuery support, and improved dynamic schema change—that reduce the effort required by developers and support staff to deliver robust DB2 applications and improve your ROI and TCO.

Hear What Our Customers Are Saying About DB2 11

Banco do Brasil—Top Bank in Brazil

"Higher availability, Performance, lower CPU consumption amongst other new features were the benefits perceived by Banco do Brasil with DB2 11 for z/OS. During our testing with DB2 11, we noticed improved performance along with stability. The archive transparency feature addresses an issue we have needed to resolve for a long time at the bank and will reduce cost. Other features that are especially beneficial to us include: Persistent thread break-in, extended RBA, APPLCOMPAT, statistics feedback, automatic index pseudo-delete cleanup, improvements in DPSI performance and utilities, and additional zIIP eligibility."

—Paulo Sahadi, IT Executive Banco do Brasil

BMW—One of the Largest Global Car Manufacturers

"We operate in a very dynamic 24/7 environment, and we often have to update our applications while they continue to operate. With DB2 11, the combination of the ability to break into persistent threads and the enhanced dynamic schema change capabilities allow us to react to business requirements more quickly and with less operational impact. We can plan, implement, and commit changes without business interruption—a major advantage for global operations."

—Peter Paetsch, BMW Group

"Despite still being very early in our performance testing, we have already seen CPU reductions of 8–13 percent on some of the workloads, thanks to the more efficient decompression algorithms that IBM DB2 allows us to run."

—Peter Paetsch, BMW Group

"IBM DB2 11 has helped us to eliminate the performance and throughput challenges associated with our business innovation plans, and we can now easily cope with our ever-growing workload."   *—Manager, BMW Group*

J N Data—Provider of IT Operations and Engineering Services to Large Danish Financial Institutions

"Running IT operations for multiple customers, like JN Data does, is challenging when doing version upgrades on DB2. All customers need to be able to upgrade their DB2 systems within a limited period of time, and if the new version contains incompatible changes for the applications, these need to be checked and recoded on all customers' systems before migration. Or they NEEDED to, because in DB2 11 a new feature isolates the need to change applications from the actual migration of the software. I predict this will make migration processes much more easy in installations like JN Data in the future."

—Frank Petersen, Systems Programmer, JN Data

"We love autonomics. DB2 11 has some really nice features for reducing the burden on the DBA, such as the automatic cleanup of pseudo-deleted index entries."   *—Frank Petersen, Systems Programmer, JN Data*

"The DB2 11 for z/OS ESP code just worked from day one, and we are looking forward to productivity gains and cost savings when we roll out live."

—Frank Petersen, Systems Programmer, JN Data

"With DB2 11, IBM is delivering the solution to the problem that more and more installations are facing: the fact that we will be running out of RBAs or perhaps even of LRSNs. The solution being delivered is truly giving us total flexibility on the path of expanding the RBAs and LRSNs, showing that IBM understands the challenges customers are facing concerning availability!"
—Frank Petersen, Systems Programmer, JN Data

Golden Living—Retirement Living Provider
"We have seen some incredible performance results with DB2 11, a major reduction of CPU time, 3.5% before rebind and nearly 5% after rebind. This will significantly bring down our operation costs. "One of the reasons I wanted to participate in the DB2 11 ESP program is because I really believe in DB2 for z/OS. I am not only a DB2 DBA, but I manage other vendor products on multiple platforms, but in my opinion, nothing compares to DB2 for z/OS for supporting mission-critical enterprise applications." *—Conrad Wolf , Golden Living*

Bank Hapoalim—Top Bank in Israel
"Extended LRSN not only resolves a technical issue but also has a positive business impact by significantly improving performance, enhancing efficiency, and reducing costs. This makes it a valuable DB2 11 feature for Bank Hapoalim. We are very pleased with the results of the extended LRSN feature—it works well and definitely addresses our pain points. The bank is very satisfied from both the ease of use and the test results."*—Guy Livni, DB2 for z/OS Team, Bank Hapoalim*

Stadtwerke—A Large Municipal Enterprise in the German Energy Market
"RECOVER of catalog and directory runs more than twice as fast as on DB2 10. The SAP IS-U unbilled revenue application (a batch workload) showed an elapsed time reduction of about 20% in conversion mode. After migration to DB2 11 new-function mode, I saw automatic index pseudo-delete cleanup, which should reduce the need to REORG after big batch runs. These enhancements will provide even more cost savings." *—Bernd Klawa, DB2 DBA, Stadtwerke*

Triton Consulting
"The new transparent archive feature promises to significantly reduce the cost of designing, developing, and testing the data archive process for DB2 for z/OS applications. We expect it to reduce developer/DBA effort by hundreds of man-hours, as well as improve coding consistency and reduce overall storage costs."
—Julian Stuhler, President, Triton Consulting

SuadaSoft—Belux Market Leader in Information Management
"In DB2 11, IBM provides an impressive list of improvements to its utilities. Whether they are overall improvements or new user choices, the DB2 11 utilities bring us more availability, better performance, more control, more cost reduction, and better day-to-day usability. It's a win-win-win as far as I'm concerned."
—Kurt Struyf, SuadaSoft

GAD eG—DP Center for German Cooperative Banks
"We have seen some really good results regarding CPU savings while running IMS-driven batch workload in our ESP test environment with DB2 11 CM/NFM. We have been so impressed with the product stability and have already moved an internal production system to DB2 11." *—Stefan Korte, GAD eG*

DB2 11 for z/OS: Technical Overview

by John Campbell and Gareth Jones

This IBM® DB2® for z/OS® white paper provides a high-level overview of the changes introduced in DB2 11 for z/OS, including the following topics:

- DB2 11 performance expectations and improvements

- Availability and resilience enhancements

- Data sharing improvements

- Security enhancements

- Utility enhancements

- Analytics improvements

- New and enhanced application features

- Easier version upgrade, including the new Application Compatibility feature

The performance expectations section concentrates on improvements that can be expected with and without REBIND and describes which improvements require DBA or application programmer effort. We discuss other features in more detail in subsequent sections.[1,2]

---

[1] Information regarding potential future products is intended to outline general product direction, and it should not be relied on in making a purchasing decision. The information mentioned regarding potential future products is not a commitment, promise, or legal obligation to deliver any material, code, or functionality. Information about potential future products might not be incorporated into any contract. The development, release, and timing of any future features or functionality described for IBM products remains at IBM's sole discretion.

[2] This document contains performance information based on measurements done in a controlled environment. The actual throughput or performance that any user experiences will vary depending upon considerations such as the amount of multiprogramming in the user's job stream, the I/O configuration, the storage configuration, and the workload processed. Therefore, no assurance can be given that an individual user can achieve throughput or performance improvements equivalent to the numbers stated here.

DB2 11 Performance Expectations

IBM recognizes that performance improvements can also result in cost savings for customers, making the IBM System z® platform more attractive and helping customer investment to deliver value.

DB2 10 for z/OS provided some significant application performance improvements by reducing CPU consumption for many online transaction processing (OLTP) applications running simple SQL queries. This theme continues in DB2 11 for z/OS, with the focus now on complex queries. In this paper, "simple queries" are queries that retrieve data using a primary key lookup; for the purposes of this discussion, you can regard all other queries as complex queries. While some performance regression for a small number of queries is possible, most DB2 11 customers can expect to see reduced CPU consumption for a significant proportion of their complex queries.

The performance improvements customers can expect from DB2 11 might vary depending on many factors. Changes to the DB2 Optimizer mean the access path chosen by the DB2 11 REBIND process could differ from that chosen by DB2 10. For example, DB2 11 can choose a nested loop join instead of a sort merge join, or vice versa. The read/write ratio is also important because DB2 11 reduces the logging overhead for write-intensive applications.

Other factors affecting performance expectations include the number of rows returned, the number and type of columns returned, the number of partitions touched, and the number of partitions defined. You are more likely to see performance improvements when using table-controlled partitioning and data-partitioned secondary indexes (DPSIs) because IBM has worked to make DPSI much more useful in this release. The BIND option RELEASE(COMMIT/DEALLOCATE) and the use of table compression are two other important factors influencing the kind of performance improvement you can expect.

Customers often want to know what enhancements they can anticipate from any new release of DB2, so it is important to be clear about which enhancements are immediately available. First, there are no Data Definition Language (DDL) changes, no Data Manipulation Language (DML) changes, and no application changes. However, this does mean that achieving the most significant performance gains for static SQL packages require a REBIND. Additional performance savings require user action in the form of DDL or DML changes or other DB2 changes.

Performance Expectations for OLTP and Batch

Table 1.1 shows the OLTP and batch CPU savings reported from IBM's own internal benchmarks. In these benchmarks, System z measures total CPU consumption—that is, the CPU consumption reported in the statistics trace as well as the accounting trace. This point is important because when you deploy DB2 11 and measure your own performance improvements, you'll need to make sure you look at the complete picture by including CPU consumption figures from both statistics and accounting.

Table 1.1: Sample CPU savings for OLTP and batch	
Workload description	CPU savings (%)
Batch running locally with a varied workload	10
Batch in a distributed environment with concurrent sequential insert processes	5
OLTP in a distributed environment executing simple SQL queries	4
OLTP running locally in a data sharing environment using the basic RBA format executing simple SQL queries	1
OLTP running locally in a data sharing environment using the extended RBA format executing simple SQL queries	4.7
Distributed OLTP running SAP banking in a data sharing environment	9
Distributed OLTP running complex queries and using SQL PL stored procedures	9.8
A set of IBM DB2 utilities	3

These figures demonstrate that positive CPU savings apply across a broad range of SQL query workloads. The modest 1 percent improvement seen for the local, non-distributed workload running simple SQL queries in a data sharing environment is expected, given that in this release IBM focused on reducing CPU consumption for complex queries. However, a healthy reduction in CPU consumption is reported for the other workloads, including the IBM utility set.

Performance Expectations for Queries

The figures in Table 1.2, representing a variety of industry-standard benchmarks and customer workloads executing complex queries, are certainly impressive. Note that these workloads include not only business intelligence but also complex OLTP and batch.

Table 1.2: DB2 11 Query workloads after REBIND without APREUSE	
Workload description	CPU savings (%)
TPC-H benchmark queries	37
TPC-H–like queries	21
Query customer workload 1	36
Query customer workload 2	36
Query customer workload 3	12
Query customer workload 4	46
Benchmark – SAP BW	33
Benchmark business intelligence, long running	47
Benchmark business intelligence, short running	14

Some of these workloads use static SQL, and for purposes of the test, the containing DB2 plans were rebound without APREUSE under DB2 11, opening up new and improved access path choices for these applications. Of course, those choices are automatically available to dynamic SQL at PREPARE time. Although most performance improvements are available even after a successful REBIND with APREUSE(ERROR) or APREUSE(WARN), you must rebind without APREUSE to get the new or improved access paths.

It is also important to understand that these are the sorts of workloads that are expected to benefit significantly from DB2 11. The savings you see might differ. Underlying the variation in CPU savings for these workloads is the fact that the functional usage of SQL varies from workload to workload; the savings you can expect will depend on the characteristics of the SQL requests issued by your applications and the design of your database schema.

DB2 11 Performance Expectations Summary

In summarizing the kind of CPU savings expected with DB2 11, you will notice we use the phrase "Up to"—which includes the value zero. For example, "Up to 10 percent for complex OLTP" should be understood as "From zero to 10 percent for complex OLTP." We discussed the reasons for this convention earlier, but, essentially, the savings you can expect are very workload-dependent.

To summarize, the total CPU savings you can expect for your SQL applications in DB2 11 are as follows:

- Up to 10 percent for complex OLTP
- Up to 10 percent for update-intensive batch
- Up to 25 percent for reporting queries without compressed tables
- Up to 40 percent for complex queries with compressed tables

Performance Highlights

In this section, we highlight some of the most significant performance improvements in DB2 11 for z/OS. Some of these might require user action, while others might not.

Two of the performance improvements can particularly help write-intensive batch applications—that is, applications that use INSERT, UPDATE, and/or DELETE intensively.

The first improvement in this area does not require REBIND because it is related to the log output buffer, which has been moved from the MSTR address space to the 64-bit common area. The advantage of this change is that DB2 now avoids a cross-memory call to the MSTR address space to update the log buffer. Avoiding these cross-memory calls reduces CPU time in particular for write-intensive applications.

The second improvement can benefit data sharing users with certain kinds of extremely write-intensive applications. It requires you to be in new-function mode (NFM). It reduces the need to spin on the CPU to obtain a new log record sequence number (LRSN). A lot of work was done in DB2 10 to reduce LRSN spins for INSERT processing, but further enhancements are available in DB2 11 if you take the necessary user actions to exploit the extended log relative byte address (RBA)/LRSN once in NFM. DB2 11 provides additional LRSN spin avoidance for UPDATE and DELETE processing and continued improvement for INSERT by greatly reducing the need for LRSN spins when updating space map pages.

Several enhancements benefit query workloads. Improving query workload performance was a primary focal point for SQL performance enhancements in DB2 11.

Applications that access compressed tables, especially those where the selected columns are clustered together or where predicates to be applied are clustered together, and where many rows are scanned, should see reduced CPU consumption because of an improved decompression algorithm.

There is also assistance for sort-intensive queries. DB2 11 reduces the need to use physical work files, generates custom machine code to use in sort processing, and improves the processing of in-memory work files. These changes not only reduce CPU consumption but also result in fewer I/O requests.

DB2 11 improves performance for queries accessing multiple DPSI partitions in a join operation where there are additional join predicates on the columns making up the partitioning key. It does this by using page range screening to ensure that only the necessary DPSI parts are accessed during the join operation.

DB2 11 includes a number of enhancements to reduce the number of data moves required and the amount of code executed when returning rows from the IBM DB2 Analytics Accelerator (IDAA). These changes are targeted mainly at queries accessing IDAA to retrieve large result sets.

Before DB2 11, queries bound with RELEASE(COMMIT), which accessed one or a small number of partitions, were sensitive to the number of partitions defined rather than the number of partitions accessed. For queries accessing tables with a large number of partitions—say more than 200—the CPU cost starts to become significant, meaning performance scales poorly as the defined number of partitions grows. However, in DB2 11, DB2 is only sensitive to the number of partitions accessed in a single COMMIT scope. The result is that the larger the number of defined partitions, the greater the performance improvement.

DB2 11 continues the theme of large real memory exploitation, delivering a further enhancement for customers using large buffer pools when running on an IBM zEnterprise® zEC12 CEC. The zEC12 provides support for page-fixed 2 GB page frames, helping to improve throughput and reduce CPU consumption when you have very large buffer pools (i.e., larger than 2 GB).

Readers might be familiar with DB2's use of runtime optimizations, or customized procedures for operations frequently used by SELECT, UPDATE, and so on, called xPROCs. DB2 11 introduces a new customized procedure for column processing that can reduce CPU consumption for queries that select a very large number of columns. The greater the number of columns selected, the greater the reduction in CPU consumption.

A significant number of DRDA, or Distributed Data Facility (DDF), applications are often described as "chatty." These long-running DDF transactions issue multiple simple SQL statements, causing a lot of send/receive TCP/IP processing in the DIST address space. Before DB2 11, DB2 used a technique called asynchronous receive in the DIST address space, which required extra supervisor request block (SRB) dispatching. With z/OS 2.1 Communications Server, or z/OS 1.13 Communications Server with APAR PM80004 applied, DB2 11 DDF replaces all asynchronous calls with synchronous calls to eliminate the SRB dispatching overhead. This change results in reduced network latency and a significant CPU reduction in the DIST address space for chatty DDF applications. No rebind is required to benefit from this change.

The enhancements we've discussed so far provide cost savings through reduced CPU consumption. This next enhancement is a simple cost saving benefit. In DB2 10, the prefetch engines and the deferred write engines became zIIP-eligible. DB2 11 extends this support by allowing all other system agents, with the exception of the P-lock negotiation agent, to become zIIP-eligible.

Two cases in particular benefit from this enhancement. First, in data sharing, DBM1 chargeable CPU time can be reduced because castout processing is eligible for zIIP offload. Second, MSTR address space chargeable CPU can also be reduced for update-intensive workloads because log read and log write are also zIIP-eligible.

ESP Customer Feedback

Several Early Support Program (ESP) customers compared the performance of DB2 11 with that of DB2 10 and sent SMF data to the DB2 Lab at IBM's Silicon Valley Lab for analysis. The measurements made using the provided data consistently indicated that performance improved once these customers had migrated to DB2 11 and rebound their static SQL packages. This fact is important because the DB2 Lab cannot possibly reproduce all customer workloads as workloads vary so widely. Due to the difficulty driving comparable online workloads, most of the customer workloads were batch. This is another significant point because, for the findings to be useful, the workloads must be comparable in terms of the SQL profile and the data being processed. It is worth noting that some customers were also able to send in SMF data for OLTP workloads, but the variety of these workloads was smaller.

The measurements from this customer SMF data were very much in line with those of the DB2 Lab. For both kinds of workloads, both batch and OLTP, CPU reduction was in the range of 5 percent to 20 percent. The data also confirmed expectations with regard to zIIP offload. Customers observed an increase in zIIP usage by the DBM1 address space in data sharing for castout processing and an increase in zIIP usage by the MSTR address space for active log write.

DB2 11 Performance Improvements in More Detail

A summary of DB2 11 performance improvement has already been provided. In the next section, we examine these and other improvements in greater detail, looking at those performance advances that:

- Are available without a REBIND

- Require a REBIND with or without APREUSE

- Require a REBIND without APREUSE

- Require DBA or application programmer effort

No REBIND Required

Although many performance improvements are available only after a REBIND, many other benefits are available immediately upon entering DB2 11 conversion mode (CM). Of course, which improvements you benefit from are determined by the characteristics of your workload.

Auto-Commit Performance Improvement

DDF performance improvements, where DB2 exploits the capabilities of the new z/OS Communications Server to reduced SRB scheduling for TCP/IP receive, have already been mentioned. This feature is available without rebind and can reduce CPU usage in the DIST address space, as well as network latency.

Steps have also been taken to improve auto-commit performance, provided your distributed OLTP applications are using IBM Data Server Driver V10.5. A feature of many read-only distributed applications is to use auto-commit to avoid managing transaction boundaries. Before this enhancement, an application of this kind using cursors could not chain a commit after a request without an additional network flow, forcing the commit request to be sent in separate flow after closing the cursor. DB2 11 provides an indicator that allows the DB2 server to initiate commit after the result set is exhausted in the initial reply to the client, reducing network flows, latency, and CPU consumption.

Continuous Block Fetch

For DRDA applications retrieving result sets with many rows, DB2 has provided support for block fetch ever since DB2 V5.1. This change reduced network traffic by sending blocks of rows in a single network message. This initial implementation, and subsequent enhancements, made this feature available to read-only cursors, to ambiguous cursors with CURRENTDATA NO, or to applications using the OPTIMIZE FOR n ROWS clause. Now, DB2 11 supports a package-based form of continuous block fetch called *blasting*, in which DB2 is both the requester and the server. Blasting is enabled by a new DBPROTOCOL setting, DRDACBF, on the BIND PACKAGE or REBIND PACKAGE command and by setting BIND option APPLCOMPAT to V11R1. A separate TCP/IP socket and DB2 database access thread (DBAT) is created for each read-only statement, and blocks of result rows are sent on the secondary connection until the result set is exhausted, when the statement is implicitly closed, and the secondary DBAT is immediately pooled. This feature is known as continuous block fetch, or blasting.

An obvious question here is, "Why is the improvement listed under 'no REBIND required'?" The answer is that packages that typically use the DISTSERV default DRDA plan, such as the DB2 CLI packages or the JDBC packages, are used by dynamic SQL applications. By exploiting this feature, any DRDA dynamic SQL applications using these packages can benefit from this feature, with the potential for reduced elapsed and CPU times, reduced network flows, and reduced network latency.

xPROC Storage

For operations that are used repeatedly, such as SELECT and UPDATE, DB2 has used runtime optimizations called customized procedures for fast column processing. For SELECT, DB2 uses a procedure called a sPROC; for UPDATE, an uPROC; and so on. These procedures are therefore known collectively as *xPROCs*. Although DB2 10 moves most statement storage above the 2 GB bar, it continues to allocate xPROCs below the bar to maintain compatibility with z/OS versions that do not support 64-bit code execution. Thus, DB2 10 has to free the storage for xPROCs that are not being used by a thread, to avoid virtual storage accumulation for unused statements.

DB2 11 provides even more virtual storage constraint relief by moving xPROCs above the 2 GB bar because z/OS 1.13 (which is a prerequisite of DB2 11) supports 64-bit code execution. Therefore, the above-the-bar xPROC storage can be allowed to persist, and DB2 11 caches xPROCs in a similar way to statements in the environmental descriptor manager (EDM) skeleton pool (for static SQL) and in the dynamic statement cache (for dynamic SQL). As well as providing 31-bit virtual storage constraint relief, this change can improve performance for commonly used statements.

As for continuous block fetch, you might wonder why this improvement is listed as not requiring rebind. There are two reasons: Dynamic SQL will benefit because the xPROCs are built at run time, and static SQL packages bound with APREUSE(ERROR) can benefit, too. While the latter condition requires REBIND, there are no access path changes.

zIIP Redirect

DB2 started exploiting the specialty zIIP engine in DB2 V8.1, with the objective of reducing total cost of ownership, especially for applications running in a distributed environment. DB2 9 and DB2 10 allowed more work to be redirected to zIIP engines, and DB2 11 continues that trend with zIIP enablement for all SRB-mode DB2 system agents (with the sole exception of the P-lock negotiation engine). Customers who have deployed zIIP engines need to plan zIIP capacity very carefully to make sure the DB2 system agents are not delayed; otherwise, this situation could lead to performance degradation. For this reason, you will need to ensure that work redirected to a zIIP engine does not then fall back to a general processor because of lack of available zIIP capacity.

Data Decompression Performance Improvement

Data compression at the table space level was implemented way back in Version 3 and is in widespread use, reducing the amount of disk space required, decreasing I/Os and GETPAGE requests, and making more efficient use of buffer pools. There is an overhead, however, as the entire data rows have to be decompressed either to apply predicates or to return the result rows to the application.

Under earlier releases, DB2 decompresses the whole row, with overhead incurred on a per-byte basis. DB2 11 introduces a very valuable optimization whereby DB2 decompresses only the portion of the row needed either for predicate evaluation or to return the columns to the application. This ability is particularly useful with long rows containing many columns, where you want to access only a small subset of the columns that are close to each other on the row. Those access paths that are data-intensive and return many columns or apply many predicates clustered together will see the best savings.

INSERT Performance

For many applications, INSERT performance is a critical factor, so DB2 11 continues the work done in DB2 9 and DB2 10 to this aspect of DB2. A number of features are important in achieving INSERT improvements.

DB2 11 reduces the potential for latch contention on latch classes 6, 14, and 19. Latch class 6 is needed for index tree splits; the buffer manager uses latch class 14; and latch class 19 is the latch on the log output buffer. Although INSERT is the main beneficiary of these changes, other SQL operations might also see performance improvements.

In addition, DB2 11 reduces the CPU required for INSERT column processing and log record creation, and it lowers the number of synchronous log writes during index structure modifications. This has been an issue for INSERT-intensive applications, particularly in data sharing.

DB2 9 and DB2 10 both included enhancements to reduce the frequency of CPU spins to obtain a unique LRSN in a data sharing environment. More details are included later about a feature you can use in new-function mode, with or without REBIND. This feature converts the log RBA and, for data sharing the LRSN, to 10 bytes. If you take the necessary actions, this change can eliminate all possibility of LRSN spin.

Automatic Index Pseudo-Delete Cleanup

Pseudo-deleted index entries have historically been a problem for some workloads because they can cause additional locks to be acquired and additional GETPAGE requests, creating not only unwanted overhead but also variability in performance. The way to deal with pseudo-deleted index entries in releases prior to DB2 11 is to use REORG INDEX or REORG TABLESPACE. This requires DBA work and the ability to schedule online REORG.

DB2 11's new autonomic feature detects index pages that have a large number of pseudo-deleted index entries and automatically cleans these up in the background. The index cleanup processing is eligible for zIIP offload, reducing the cost of this operation and avoiding unwanted scheduling of the REORG utility.

To help manage the possible overheads of the cleanup process—including CPU overhead, disruption to other concurrent threads, and an increase in logging volume—the DBA can control the process via the INDEX_CLEANUP_THREADS subsystem parameter and the SYSIBM.SYSINDEXCLEANUP catalog table.

We discuss automatic index pseudo-delete cleanup in more detail later in this paper.

DPSI Performance Improvements

The use case for data-partitioned secondary indexes has been limited by a number of performance considerations. DB2 11 features several performance enhancements in this area, and while other enhancements require a REBIND, the DPSI merger improvements are available automatically. DPSI merge is one strategy DB2 uses to avoid a sort when returning rows in order using a DPSI. To do this, DB2 processes each partition serially, but a merge process returns the result in order across all partitions. Improved index look-aside, resulting in fewer GETPAGE requests, and other enhancements deliver significant performance improvements for queries using DPSIs.

RELEASE(DEALLOCATE) Performance Optimization

One of the tasks for this release was to try to optimize RELEASE(DEALLOCATE) performance so that it consistently performs better than RELEASE(COMMIT). With the rollout of DB2 10 and 64-bit storage exploitation, many customers are making much more use of persistent threads, such as CICS protected entry threads and IMS WFI regions, and making much more widespread use of RELEASE(DEALLOCATE). In most cases, that use is a performance winner and a very big performance opportunity. However, in a few cases, it's possible to accumulate a lot of parent locks and internal storage structures for long-lived persistent threads, causing excessive storage usage and CPU overhead. DB2 11 introduces an internal threshold that lets DB2 detect whether storage has accumulated unnecessarily for unneeded parent locks and internal storage structures and then purges those locks and structures.

IFI 306 Filtering Capabilities to Improve Replication Capture Performance

IFCID 306 is the record used by replication products and programs to capture update information from the DB2 log for tables that are replicated locally or remotely. DB2 11 introduces IFI filtering that lets the consumer of IFCID 306 provide filtering information to ensure that DB2 passes it log records only for the subset of DB2 objects it is interested in. This filtering has the potential to dramatically improve the performance of replication capture. However, it requires some enhancements and probably new releases of whichever replication tool you use. For example, IBM InfoSphere® Change Data Capture (CDC) must be upgraded to Version 10.2.1.

ACCESS DATABASE Command Performance

The ACCESS DATABASE command is used to open data sets before applications need them to avoid incurring the associated overhead when the applications are started. The situations where this can be useful include a disaster recovery event, DB2 restart after a system crash, or the restart of applications after they have been quiesced. Previously, the ACCESS DATABASE command would open the data sets serially, causing elongated elapsed command execution time. The DB2 11 enhancement, which has also been retrofitted to DB2 10, causes an ACCESS DATABASE command with a string of objects to open to process the OPEN requests in parallel. This enhancement has generated amazing elapsed time improvements, which might make the use of this command more attractive to a wider set of customers, as well as to those who already use the ACCESS DATABASE command.

DGTT Performance Improvements

Many applications use declared global temporary tables (DGTTs), and even when accessed via static SQL package, statements accessing DGTTs are actually processed dynamically. This activity shows up in DB2 accounting and statistics trace records in the form of incremental binds, and these incremental binds will result in prepares. DB2 11 removes this requirement for applications bound with RELEASE(DEALLOCATE). This is a key point: This change applies only to RELEASE(DEALLOCATE), and it means

DB2 can avoid the need for the incremental bind and therefore PREPARE. PREPARE can be CPU-intensive, so incremental bind avoidance delivers reduced CPU overhead.

IBM zEnterprise zEC12 Exploitation

DB2 11 continues the theme established by previous DB2 releases of exploiting IBM zSeries hardware and z/OS. DB2 11 focuses on making the best use of the new features of the zEC12 CEC.

The zEC12 supports 2 GB real storage page frames. DB2's intended use of this feature is when individual buffer pools are 2 GB in size or more. The advantage of this is that a greater amount of the DB2 working set can be represented in what is called the *translation look-aside buffer (TLB)*. z/OS uses the TLB for dynamic address translation (DAT) when translating virtual storage addresses into real storage addresses, thereby avoiding misses in the TLB and reducing CPU consumption.

For customers who have Flash Express installed and configured, DB2 can use pageable 1 MB size page frames for the buffer pool control structures—not the buffers themselves, but the buffer pool control structures. If you are also using z/OS 2.1, DB2 can use 1 MB size page frames for the DB2 code itself.

It is important to stress that Flash Express is not a replacement for or an alternative to real storage. Flash Express is a faster device for paging than traditional auxiliary storage. For a high-performance DB2 system, avoid paging either to Flash Express or to auxiliary storage.

As a more general point, DB2 Development continues to strive to make sure that a single DB2 subsystem can scale effectively with IBM's largest n-way processors, and to that end a number of changes have been made in DB2 11 latch management to reduce contention, plus a number of other scalability improvements.

Data Sharing Performance Improvements

DB2 11 brings some very welcome improvements for data sharing customers, in the areas of castout and index split.

Write-intensive applications can suffer performance problems when changed pages are written to the group buffer pool (GBP) faster than the castout engines can process them. This can lead to a very high percentage of the GBP being congested with changed pages that have not been written out to DASD, and in extreme cases a GBP full condition. To relieve this sort of problem, DB2 11 tries to overlap the operations for read for castout (from the GBP into DBM1 storage belonging to the castout owner) with those for castout writes to disk. This behavior results in a shorter wait time for castout I/O completion and reduces the stress on GBP pages.

DB2 11 introduces another feature, called *group buffer pool write-around*, to deal with the situation where intensive, sustained GBP page-write activity results in changed pages dominating the group buffer pool, leading to write failures and pages being placed on the logical page list (LPL), thus impacting application performance and availability. Group buffer pool write-around uses a feature called *conditional write* to avoid writing pages to the GBP by writing them directly to DASD instead, while still using the GBP to perform cross-invalidation. DB2 automatically detects when writes are flooding the GBP and dynamically switches to using GBP write-around for those objects that are causing the heaviest write activity. Once the condition has been relieved, DB2 returns to normal GBP write activity.

The pages that are eligible for GBP write-around are those that are written asynchronously from the local buffer pool to the group buffer pool via deferred write where the pages do not already exist in the GBP. GBP writes resulting from COMMIT or index split are synchronous writes and therefore do not qualify for group buffer pool write-around.

Index leaf page split processing in a data sharing environment where the index object is GBP-dependent can cause significant performance problems. DB2 Development has made a series of improvements over recent releases of DB2 to optimize index leaf page split performance. In DB2 11, IBM has reduced the number of force writes to the log and the number of writes to the group buffer pool that are required for an index leaf page split. Depending particularly on the intensity of INSERT processing, the benefits can be quite significant.

REBIND Required—With or Without APREUSE

DB2 10 introduced the ability for customers to try to ensure that, for static SQL, the Optimizer chooses the same access path as found in the already existing package during rebind, through use of the APREUSE (access path reuse) option on BIND and REBIND. The enhancements described in this section are available if REBIND is successful whether or not APREUSE is specified, because the REBIND process itself delivers these changes simply by building new executable structures.

Query Transformation Improvements

DB2 11 includes a number of query transformation improvements with the aim of making fewer demands for programmer expertise in writing efficient SQL and providing the Optimizer with better access path choices.

The first of these improvements is enhanced query rewrite to improve predicate indexability. There are now more cases where the Optimizer can rewrite non-indexable predicates to make them indexable. In addition, some commonly used predicates that used to be stage 2 are now rewritten by the Optimizer so that they are now indexable, stage 1 predicates. For example:

```
YEAR(), DATE(), SUBSTR(col,1,x), value BETWEEN COL1 AND COL2
```

Query rewrite also provides improved indexability for predicates such as OR COL IS NULL, and it pushes some of the more complex predicates into materialized views and table expressions by adding query rewrite support for some further stage 2 predicates, non-Boolean term predicates, and ON clause predicates. CASE predicates can also be indexable.

In addition, in the case once again of non-Boolean term predicates, correlated subqueries can now be converted to non-correlated where there is a local predicate, even across all legs of UNION or UNION ALL.

The Optimizer has been further enhanced for more efficient pruning of always-true and always-false predicates, such as WHERE 1 = 1 or WHERE 2 = 3, to solve the problem where predicates like these restrict the choices available to the Optimizer, leading to the selection of poorer access paths. Complex OR predicates with an always-false condition such as WHERE (COLA = :HV OR 1 = 2) are simplified, with the exception of 0 = 1 because that particular predicate is a commonly used technique, and removing support for it would cause problems for many applications.

Once more, in the area of predicate pushdown, stage 2 predicates can now be pushed down for data row evaluation during data page list prefetch.

Enhanced Duplicate Removal

Many queries require duplicate removal, such as queries using DISTINCT and GROUP BY. These duplicate elimination processes have traditionally used DB2 sort, which can be expensive. DB2 11 reduces the cost by introducing two new techniques.

The first technique uses the index to skip over duplicates. The second, called *early out*, involves early detection of whether a candidate row is a duplicate. If the row is a duplicate, it can be eliminated immediately from further processing. Both of these techniques apply to some instances of DISTINCT and GROUP BY, but not all, meaning that in some cases a sort is still be required.

The latter change does not show up in PLAN_TABLE. To work out whether a sort was required, you can check the IXSCAN_SKIP_DUPS, IXSCAN_SKIP_SCREEN, and EARLY_OUT columns in the DSN_DETCOST_TABLE to determine whether a sort was avoided.

In-Memory Techniques

DB2 11 expands the use of in-memory, reusable work files in join processing. These work files are often referred to as the *in-memory data cache*. The amount of memory used by the cache is controlled by the MXDTCACH ZPARM. DB2 11 also opens up the use of sparse index, which is used when insufficient memory exists for the in-memory data cache. Non-correlated subqueries can now exploit the in-memory data cache, and it can also be used to cache correlated subquery results.

Additional Performance Improvements

There is a long list of additional performance improvements that require a REBIND, which are all worthy of mention:

- We have already discussed xPROCs, which facilitate fast column processing. REBIND generates some unique, customized machine code for output column processing. On a more general note, the non-xPROC machine instructions for input and output column processing have also been optimized.

- DB2 10 avoided the significant cost of row ID (RID) processing failures by allowing RIDs to overflow to a work file. DB2 11 extends this functionality even further by including RID overflow support for Data Manager set functions (COUNT, MAX, MIN, and so on).

- DB2 11 provides performance improvements for common operators such as MOVE, CAST, CASE, SUBSTR, DATE, and others.

- The DECFLOAT data type was introduced primarily to help Java® applications. Performance here has improved substantially, with up to a 23 percent CPU reduction for conversion to and from DECFLOAT and up to around 50 percent CPU reduction for INSERT and FETCH for DECFLOAT columns. This has been helped further by zEC12 hardware improvements for decimal floating point.

- Better performance is delivered for non-correlated subqueries where there is a length mismatch.

- Non-column expressions in a select list can be executed once per query rather than for every qualifying row. This feature is known as *select list do-once*.

REBIND Required—Without APREUSE

Continuing the theme of performance improvements that require a REBIND, some improvements in DB2 11 are obtained only by a change in access path, which means REBIND without APREUSE.

Two enhancements in this area apply to data partitioned secondary indexes. First, page range screening, so that only qualified index partitions are accessed, is available for join and correlation predicates. Second, DPSI nested loop join is improved by introducing parallelism in which each child task processes one DPSI part. Parallelism is also improved, with ZPARM PARAMDEG_DPSI controlling the degree of parallelism.

Back in DB2 V9.1, IBM recognized that the introduction of faster processors meant that the relative weights given to CPU and I/O when calculating access path costs were becoming unbalanced as processor speeds became faster, and it introduced the OPTIOWGT ZPARM to address that particular problem. DB2 11 takes a further step in this direction, this time with no special ZPARM to control the improvement. The objective is to reduce the number of cases where the Optimizer favors access paths with more I/O overhead over those consuming more CPU. Our internal workloads have seen positive changes in access path selection, delivering an elapsed time improvement of between 3 percent and 30 percent for our query workloads.

DBA or Application Programmer Effort Required

As with all DB2 releases, a number of enhancements in DB2 11 require not only a REBIND but also effort from the DBA or application programmer to exploit.

The first of these is the introduction of "suppress-null" indexes. With this type of index, index entries are not created when the value for all indexed columns is NULL. For tables with a large number of such rows, suppress-null indexes provide a number of benefits, including reduced index size, improved insert/update/delete performance, improved utility performance, and improved CREATE INDEX performance. For portability, this feature provides compatibility with other DBMSs.

For tables with varying-length columns, changes in row size can present a problem when an updated row can no longer fit in its original page, leading to indirect references, degraded data row clustering, and unwanted GETPAGE requests. A new PCTFREE FOR UPDATE table space attribute can reduce the number of indirect references and can mean fewer table space reorganizations.

A longstanding customer requirement has been for declared global temporary table performance improvements. As already discussed, incremental bind and prepare avoidance help in this area. For applications that use DGTTs as a temporary workspace, where logging is an unwanted overhead, additional benefit is delivered by the introduction of not-logged DGTTs, which can have the beneficial side effect of reducing overall logging volume.

To allow easier, more efficient sharing of data among SQL statements, DB2 11 introduces global variables. Global variables allow values to be shared across all SQL statements within the same connection.

Data sharing customers are always keen for performance improvements in this area, and one of the most anticipated is further LRSN spin reduction after migration to use the extended LRSN. We cover this topic in more detail later, but in terms of performance, this improvement means less stress contention on the log latch, fewer wasted CPU cycles, and improved performance, in particular for insert-intensive applications.

We discuss the next two items in more detail later, but we mention them briefly here because they are important REBIND-required features.

Most customers are familiar with the difficulty in understanding what statistics to collect, so that the Optimizer can choose the best access path. This challenge applies just as much to packaged applications as to proprietary ones. To provide assistance, the Optimizer can now identify missing or conflicting statistics during bind/prepare and externalize those. DBA skills or tooling are required to convert this output into input for RUNSTATS.

To improve customer ability to influence access path selection for tables with unusual data demographics, DB2 11 introduces extended optimization. This feature can be used to generate your own selectivity overrides—in other words, filter factor hints. This enhancement is really for the expert or for vendor tooling products; the objective is to improve the ability of the Optimizer to find the cheapest access path. Filter factor information can be added to a selectivity profile that can be exploited by BIND QUERY and then used by BIND, REBIND, and PREPARE to hopefully select a better access path.

DB2-Related Enhancements in z/OS 2.1

As always, DB2 enhancements go hand in hand with z/OS, and it should come as no surprise that benefits are available to customers running DB2 11 with z/OS V2.1.

There has been a steady growth of interest in DB2 system-level backup, via the BACKUP SYSTEM utility, which uses IBM FlashCopy® at the DASD volume level. To improve usability, you can now recover a single table space from a DB2 system-level backup even if the DASD volume where the object originally resided no longer has sufficient space and therefore a different volume has to be used. Alongside this, if the system-level backup is staged onto tape, you can also restore a table space onto a different target volume.

In the same area, the BACKUP SYSTEM utility can use FlashCopy consistency groups.

In what is currently a z/OS-only enhancement, support for Remote Direct Memory Access (RDMA) is introduced. This feature is intended to reduce the size of the TCP/IP stack and to reduce latency between distributed application servers and DB2. Because RDMA is for z/OS only, the number of applications likely to benefit currently is quite small. This enhancement also requires new hardware, which is available with zEC12 GA2.

With z/OS 2.1, IBM Data Facility Storage Management Subsystem (DFSMS) introduces StorageTiers, which optimizes data set placement for both hard disk drives (HDD) and solid state drives (SSD). DB2 support is provided using a new Instrumentation Facility Interface (IFI) command that allows DFSMS to close the data set and move it to a better-performing location, on either HDD or SSD.

Buffer Pool Enhancements

DB2 9 started using a most-recently-used (MRU) algorithm to manage sequential reads by the COPY utility. The intention was to improve buffer-hit ratio, reducing I/O by avoiding the displacement of useful random pages by pages read into the buffer pool by the COPY utility. The success of this change means that the use of MRU is extended in DB2 11 to other utilities that perform sequential reads.

Buffer pool tuning remains an important task for most customers, and understanding the buffer pool hit ratio and setting the VPSEQT threshold can be quite difficult. DB2 9 complicated this task by stopping pages read in sequentially from being reclassified later as random pages. With DB2 11, pages read into the buffer pool by dynamic prefetch or by list prefetch, and pages read sequentially into the buffer pool for format writes, remain classified as sequential. However, when a random GETPAGE touches one of these sequential pages, that page is now reclassified as random and is removed from the sequential LRU chain. This action produces two useful effects: The accuracy of random hit ratio statistics is improved, and in many cases the reclassification also improves buffer pool hit ratios by protecting random pages from buffer pool page steal.

DB2 10 introduced support for 1 MB size real storage page frames and used those 1 MB size page frames where possible for buffer pools that already used the page fix buffer pool attribute, PGFIX. The PGFIX attribute was introduced in DB2 V8.1 to avoid the overhead of fixing and freeing pages with every I/O operation. This meant that to gain the benefit of large page frames, you had to page-fix your buffer pools.

So what benefit do large page frames provide? Well, they reduce the CPU overhead of dynamic address translation by avoiding lookup misses in the translation look-aside buffer. The zEC12 extends this advantage by providing support for 2 GB size real storage page frames, and DB2 11 exploits this support with a new FRAMESIZE attribute on the -ALTER BUFFERPOOL command that lets you select a 4 KB, 1 MB, or 2 GB real storage page frame size. This enhancement is important because it divorces the selection of the real storage page frame size from the decision about whether to use page fixing.

The use of 2 GB size page frames is really targeted at customers who have large or very large buffer pools—that is, individual buffer pools that are at least 2 GB in size. Not only do 2 GB size page frames require the zEC12, but these page frames also require z/OS V2.1.

The final point in this section will be helpful for those customers who are using Workload Manager (WLM)-managed buffer pools—in other words, those who have enabled AUTOSIZE. Before this enhancement, buffer pools were allowed to grow by up to 25 percent between DB2 restart and stop. However, if the system was recycled, they could grow by another 25 percent in the next restart–stop cycle. If uncontrolled, WLM-managed buffer pools could simply keep on increasing in size across DB2 restarts. DB2 11 addresses this issue by adding two new buffer pool attributes,

VPSIZEMIN and VPSIZEMAX, which specify, respectively, the minimum and maximum allowable number of buffers. Of course, these values are honored across DB2 restarts.

Query Performance and Management Improvements

We've already discussed some of the query performance and management improvements; this section goes into more detail on some of these items, which include:

- Optimizer externalization of missing or conflicting statistics

- Support for APREUSE(WARN)

- DPSI performance improvements

Optimizer Externalization of Missing or Conflicting Statistics

The DB2 Optimizer is a cost-based SQL query optimizer, and in order for it to make the right decision, it's important for the right statistics to be collected, on both the tables and the indexes. Working out what statistics to gather is often a problem for many customers, especially if they have packaged applications or many objects to manage. Therefore, most of them just gather the default statistics, which means RUNSTATS TABLESPACE or RUNSTATS INDEX with KEYCARD. Since DB2 10, the KEYCARD option was on by default, and as of DB2 11 it is deprecated, as you can no longer turn it off.

However, an examination of past query performance Problem Management Records (PMRs) raised with the DB2 Lab shows that more than 50 percent of these issues were solved by collecting the right statistics. Following further research, estimates are that most customers would save more than 10 percent CPU if better statistics were available. To help solve the problem of how to decide which statistics to gather, DB2 11 now tries to identify whether any missing or conflicting statistics are preventing the Optimizer from making a better decision. This information is externalized so that the skilled DBA or vendor tooling can analyze that information and then modify RUNSTATS to improve the quality of the collected statistics.

Figure 1.1 illustrates, at a high level, the process the Optimizer goes through during BIND, REBIND, and PREPARE processing when deciding which access path to select for any given query. DB2 uses statistics stored in the DB2 Catalog plus information from the Real-Time Statistics (RTS) tables, together with some in-memory information. But, if the Optimizer identifies some missing or conflicting statistics, it asynchronously writes this information into the new SYSSTATFEEDBACK table. That information can then be exploited by tooling, or by a DB2 expert, to generate modified RUNSTATS requests.

The process for EXPLAIN is very similar, with information about any missing or conflicting statistics being written synchronously to a new explain table, DSN_STAT_FEEDBACK, which can also be used to generate modified RUNSTATS options so that more useful statistics are collected.

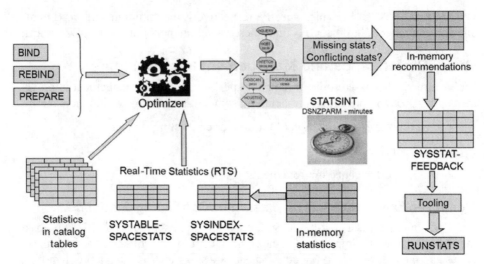

Figure 1.1: Illustration of the high-level process used by the Optimizer during BIND, REBIND, and PREPARE processing when deciding which access path to select for a given query.

APREUSE(WARN)

Having been adversely affected by access path changes in the past, many customers welcomed the support introduced in DB2 10 with the APREUSE(ERROR) option on BIND and REBIND, which asked the Optimizer to build new runtime structures but reuse the existing access path. However, if one or more SQL statements inside that SQL package failed to get the same access path, the entire BIND or REBIND request would fail.

DB2 11 introduces the APREUSE(WARN) option for BIND and REBIND. When option APREUSE(WARN) is specified, the Optimizer tries to reuse the existing access path, but if that attempt fails for a given statement, it generates a new access path for that specific statement and allows the BIND or REBIND to succeed. This support effectively introduces access path reuse at the statement level.

Here is what APREUSE(WARN) and APREUSE(ERROR) actually do: They extract information about the previous access path from information stored inside the existing package and exploit the optimization hints infrastructure to generate access path hints, which are used to generate a new run time.

The clear advantage of APREUSE(WARN), particularly on use of BIND REPLACE on application upgrade, is that if one or more statements fail to get the old access path, the Optimizer does not give up. Instead, it generates a new run time with a new access path for those statements that fail, and it issues warning messages to explain what happened.

DPSI Improvements

The goal in DB2 11 is to improve query performance for DPSIs such that you can safely replace some non-partitioned indexes (NPIs) with DPSIs and use them in many more situations. DPSIs have been very useful for utility processing, but the application use case for DPSI is quite restricted. Therefore, in this release of DB2, IBM is trying to broaden that application use case.

First, CPU parallelism on partition boundaries is now available for joins into DPSIs. DB2 11 also allows I/O parallelism for single-table DPSI access.

Next, DB2 11 introduces page range screening for join predicates so that only the qualified partitions are accessed during the join operation. Join performance is further improved by implementing a partition-level join with sequential access to the inner table.

Last, two enhancements avoid sort when using DPSIs. In addition to being able to avoid sort with regular indexes, DB2 11 can now avoid sort when using index on expression. Index look-aside also provides opportunities for sort avoidance.

Availability Improvements

DB2 for z/OS has always been the leading database management system (DBMS) for high availability, but in this release it continues to make some significant improvements in this area. The topics discussed here are:

* Extended RBA/LRSN

* BIND, REBIND, DDL, and online REORG concurrency for persistent threads using packages bound with RELEASE(DEALLOCATE)

* More online schema changes

Extended RBA and LRSN

Two important factors are behind the decision to expand the log relative byte address and the log record sequence umber in data sharing, which is based on the system clock. First, some customers have already encountered a situation where the 6-byte RBA is no longer big enough, and they've had to go through a process of resetting the RBA, which involves a DB2 subsystem outage that is particularly painful in a non-data sharing environment. Second, some data sharing customers are in danger of wrapping the LRSN. This can happen where a customer has converted from non-data sharing to data sharing, and because the LRSN must always be higher than the RBA, a delta is applied to the LRSN, which pushes the LRSN value into some virtual date in the future. It was therefore important that DB2 11 extended both the RBA and the LRSN addressing range so as to avoid the significant impact of running out of RBA or wrapping the LRSN.

DB2 11 delivers a non-disruptive solution by expanding the log RBA and the LRSN value from 6 bytes to 10 bytes, which the customer can implement gradually after reaching new-function mode.

So, first, this provides a massive increase in RBA capacity, such that a single DB2 subsystem can log up to 1 yottabyte, which represents 1,024 bytes. To put this into perspective, this amounts to about 30 times more than the estimated total amount of digital data that will be in existence worldwide by the year 2020.

The LRSN is extended by 1 byte on the left and 3 bytes on the right. The 3-byte extension provides 16,000,000 more times precision, effectively eliminating the LRSN spin problem. The 1-byte extension means it would take 30,000 years to exhaust the LRSN. The decision to extend the LRSN to 10 bytes instead of 8 bytes is intended to solve all foreseeable LRSN spin problems and also provide enough capacity for the future.

It's important to note that DB2 11 in all modes—conversion mode, enabling-new-function mode (ENFM), and new-function mode—operates internally using the 10-byte log RBA/LRSN value. But externally, messages, utility output, and input to utilities such as RECOVER will continue to use 6-byte values in conversion mode. Once in new-function mode, DB2 continues to use 6-byte values externally until you, the user, take some action to convert to the extended RBA or LRSN values.

To convert to using the extended RBA or LRSN, there are two optional tasks that can be done in any order. First to mention is the action to convert the bootstrap data sets to a new format, which enables logging with the larger RBA/LRSN values. Second, you can convert the pagesets themselves, including the catalog and directory, to a new page format that supports the extended RBA or LRSN values.

Remember, these tasks are optional, and if you aren't yet concerned with wrapping the RBA or LRSN addressing range, and you don't have any performance issues related to LRSN spin, there's no need for you to start the conversion process. There's no deadline to complete conversion, and if you do start conversion, you can do this at your leisure. The bootstrap data set (BSDS) can be converted without converting the pagesets, and you can convert the pagesets before converting the BSDS. You can convert the pagesets in a piecemeal fashion over many months, or even years. However, there is a performance advantage in converting the bootstrap data sets first, which is the recommended best practice.

BIND, REBIND, DDL, and Online REORG Break-in with Persistent Threads

This next topic is probably the most important availability enhancement in this release: the ability to allow BIND, REBIND, DDL, and online REORG to break into persistent threads that are running packages bound with RELEASE(DEALLOCATE) when those threads commit. Because of the 31-bit virtual storage constraint relief delivered by DB2 10, many more customers are making use of persistent threads, using such mechanisms as IMS pseudo-WFI regions or CICS protected ENTRY threads with RELEASE(DEALLOCATE) packages. The problem is that certain types of operation that include BIND, REBIND, DDL, and certain types of online REORG, such as those that materialize changes that cause package invalidation, cannot break in because of the package locks in share mode held by these threads.

To solve this problem, DB2 11 delivers a new break-in mechanism. DB2 now automatically detects the fact that operations are waiting for the package lock held by RELEASE(DEALLOCATE) packages and breaks in at the next COMMIT. Effectively, DB2 temporarily changes the behavior of these packages to that of RELEASE(COMMIT). Once the operation, such as BIND or REBIND, has been completed, the packages resume normal RELEASE(DEALLOCATE) behavior. The new mechanism is controlled by a new, online changeable ZPARM, PKGREL_COMMIT. The parameter's default value is YES, so this described behavior is on by default.

This is a really exciting enhancement from an availability viewpoint. The enhancement allows functions such as REBIND SWITCH, BIND REPLACE, or online REORGs that materialize pending changes and invalidate packages to break in successfully. The clear advantage is that you no longer need to shut down applications to perform these sorts of operations.

There are some cases where this break-in mechanism does not apply. For example, if you have a WITH HOLD cursor that is still open when COMMIT is issued, if COMMIT is issued inside a stored procedure, or if a package is bound with KEEPDYNAMIC(YES), then the old restrictions as per RELEASE(COMMIT) still apply.

Online Schema Changes

DB2 11 continues to make strides forward with a number of enhancements to online schema change.

The first enhancement is online ALTER for partition limit keys. Before DB2 11, affected partitions were set to REORG-pending (REORP) status, which meant that those partitions could not be accessed until you ran REORG to redistribute the data, removing the status and making the data available once again. In DB2 11 NFM, ALTER of the limit key is treated as a pending alter. The affected partitions are no longer set to REORP status; rather, the partitions are set to advisory REORG (AREOR) status, and the data in the partitions remains available. You must run online REORG to materialize the pending changes.

Only certain types of table spaces are supported. Universal table space (UTS) partitioned by range is supported, as is the classic partitioned table space, provided the classic partitioned table spaces uses table-controlled partitioning.

The new limit keys are materialized in the SYSIBM.SYSTABLEPART catalog table in the SWITCH phase. Some restrictions apply where the tables involved are referred to by materialized query tables (MQTs), have field procedures, have DB2-enforced referential integrity links, contain triggers, or have index on expression indexes defined on them.

A longstanding requirement is to provide support for DROP COLUMN, which is another kind of pending ALTER. When ALTER ... DROP COLUMN is issued, the table space is put into advisory REORG-pending status, but the data remains available. When the materializing REORG is run, the column is dropped, and the data from that column is no longer available. Be aware that REORG can materialize DROP COLUMN only if the entire table space is reorganized; you cannot do this partition by partition. DROP COLUMN is supported only for UTS.

There are some side effects of this operation. REORG will invalidate all packages referencing the table. Point-in-time recovery is not allowed to a point in time before the successful materializing REORG. To record this restriction, a record is inserted into SYSCOPY with an ICTYPE of A for alter, an STYPE of C for column, and a TTYPE of D for drop.

RAS Improvements

Next is quite a long list of reliability, availability, and serviceability (RAS) improvements. Although we describe some of these features only briefly, they can deliver significant value to customers.

The first RAS enhancement is the ability to forcibly cancel DDF threads, using a new FORCE option on the CANCEL DDF THREAD command. For the command to work, you must have first tried to cancel the thread without the FORCE option. This new option applies only to DDF threads and has as a prerequisite z/OS APAR OA39392, which is available for z/OS V1.13 and later.

Also in this area is an improvement to the DRDA SQLCancel() flow, which now causes an interrupt even when waiting on locks, executing stored procedures, or forwarding a statement on to another DB2.

For customers with many pagesets, the open data set limit has been doubled to 200,000. This enhancement has been retrofitted to DB2 10 via APAR.

To control sort processing, you can use the new ZPARM MAXSORT_IN_MEMORY to specify the maximum storage a sort can use. This setting applies at the thread level, and you can specify values between 1 MB and 128 MB. The default is 1 MB, the same value used internally in DB2 10.

Hybrid join is restricted so that it can no longer use all the RID pool storage but is instead limited to 80 percent.

DB2 adjusts the degree of query parallelism based on available system resources, to prevent an excessive number of parallel tasks causing system availability problems. Also in this area, DB2 11 allows for more robust virtual storage allocation to avoid overruns.

A new MODE(STATS) option on the ACCESS DATABASE command lets you force externalization on demand of Real-Time Statistics. This ability can be useful, for example, if you have procedures that rely on these statistics to drive utility processing.

Here are some additional performance-monitoring enhancements:

- zIIP CPU time has been added to the CPU trace header.

- Accounting trace class 10 package detail is now included in a package accounting rollup.

- "Not accounted for" time for query parallelism is reduced.

- Accumulated transaction summary data is now available by connection type, with new IFCID 369.

- More granular stored procedure and user-defined function monitoring is provided, with this enhancement being retrofitted to DB2 10 via APAR.

- Another feature, discussed already, that fits into this category is the new function to externalize information about missing or conflicting statistics into a catalog or explain table. You can use this information, probably with the assistance of tooling, to generate new RUNSTATS options for the affected objects.

- Fast log apply during DB2 restart, which was accidentally disabled during the life of DB2 9, is re-enabled by DB2 11.

- You can now use SQL SELECT against both SPT01 and DBD01, something customers have asked for.

- The DESCSTAT option, which controls whether DB2 builds an SQL descriptor area (SQLDA) when binding static SQL statements and was previously available as a ZPARM, is now a BIND option to provide control at the individual package level.

- There are new administration stored procedures to issue z/OS commands, improving manageability.

- IFCID 306 is enhanced so that the version of a compression dictionary as it was prior to a REORG is available to applications that read the DB2 log. An example of this sort of application is IBM InfoSphere Change Data Capture.

Autonomic Index Pseudo-Delete Cleanup

We briefly discussed autonomic index pseudo-delete cleanup earlier in this paper. Here, we provide more details, given the level of interest in this item.

If pseudo-deleted index entries are allowed to accumulate, they increase the number of GETPAGE requests, the number of lock requests, and the overall CPU cost of SQL statements. They can also cause query performance variability and unpredictability and, perhaps worse, can lead to deadlocks or timeouts for update applications.

Before DB2 11, DB2 included functionality that tried to autonomically clean up pseudo-deleted index entries and pseudo-empty index pages. However, in many cases this attempt was unsuccessful, requiring customers to run the REORG INDEX utility or reorganize the indexes as part of a REORG TABLESPACE operation to completely remove the pseudo-deleted index entries or pseudo-empty index pages.

New function in DB2 11 automatically cleans up index pages containing pseudo-deleted index entries and pseudo-empty pages as they are referenced. This cleanup processing is eligible for zIIP offload. This function is designed to have minimal disruption on your workload. To assist you, DB2 11 provides a new ZPARM to control the number of cleanup tasks, which defaults to 10.

There is also a new catalog table, SYSINDEXCLEANUP, that gives you the ability to control cleanup processing at the individual index level. By default, this new autonomic function is on permanently, 24 hours a day, and is applied to all indexes. SYSINDEXCLEANUP lets you exclude individual indexes from pseudo-deleted entry cleanup. Because many customers might to want to control autonomic pseudo-deleted entry cleanup for many, if not all, of their indexes, SYSINDEXCLEANUP enables this control on an index-by-index basis. You can control, by day of week or month and by time of day, when cleanup runs.

As well as resulting in fewer GETPAGE requests, improved SQL performance, and a reduced need to run the REORG INDEX utility, autonomic pseudo-delete cleanup can decrease the size of some indexes because the index pages are no longer populated by large numbers of pseudo-deleted index entries.

Reduction of Overflow Rows and Indirect References

The reduction of overflow rows and indirect references is another topic already discussed briefly but described in more detail here.

The problem here is that an update to a variable-length or compressed row can cause the row to increase in size and stop it from fitting back into its "home" data page. When this happens, DB2 moves the new version of the row to another data page and replaces the original row with a pointer record. Any index entries remain unchanged and continue to refer to the original row. This is what is meant by an *indirect reference*. This situation can cause significant performance problems because it can often result in additional I/O even worse, it can cause sequential processing to degrade to random I/O.

The REORGNEARINDREF and REORGFARINDREF columns of the SYSTABLESPACESTATS Real-Time Statistics table can help you can detect indirect references, but the only way to clean this up is to run the REORG TABLESPACE utility.

To help avoid this undesirable situation, DB2 11 provides a DDL enhancement called PCTFREE FOR UPDATE. This option reserves additional free space on top of the already existing PCTFREE to handle the update of varying length or compressed rows. PCTFREE is honored by both LOAD and REORG, but not by INSERT. The new PCTFREE FOR UPDATE attribute is honored not only by LOAD and REORG but also by INSERT. This leaves additional free space for UPDATE to extend the length of a row.

Zero, the default value for PCTFREE FOR UPDATE, is the current behavior. If you want to use this feature, there are two available choices. You can either specify your own particular value for PCTFREE FOR UPDATE, or you can specify PCTFREE FOR UPDATE -1, which asks DB2 to work out the best value during REORG processing by using Real-Time Statistics information. If you choose the latter option—which is the recommended one—it's important to run a REORG immediately afterward to enable DB2 to collect the right information to make a well-informed decision.

DDF Enhanced Client Information Fields

Distributed Data Facility (DDF) client information fields are already available today, and they provide a very useful tool for fine-grained monitoring, reporting, and managing of DDF workloads. DB2 11 enhances this capability by providing larger, longer fields, which are tolerated in conversion mode and exploited in new-function mode.

These longer fields are supported in accounting records, traces, messages, and displays. They can be used by the Resource Limit Facility to control the resources used by distributed SQL statements, and by System Profile Monitoring in, for example, identifying problem SQL statements. The z/OS Workload Manager can also use the extended client information fields for workload classification.

A new client information field, CLIENT_CORR_TOKEN, enables end-to-end monitoring of business processes all the way from the application server through to the DB2 for z/OS server. There is also a new built-in session variable that identifies the client IP address, which can be used to supplement or as an alternative to other client information fields.

Data Sharing Improvements

DB2 11 provides a host of data sharing improvements. The first of these, called group buffer pool write-around, is intended to avoid problems where the group buffer pool becomes flooded with changed pages. (We discussed this feature from a performance point of view earlier in this paper). This situation can lead to GBP write failures, resulting in processing delays and, ultimately, to pages being added to the logical page list, meaning these pages are unavailable, potentially affecting application availability.

Using group buffer pool write-around for asynchronous writes, DB2 performs a conditional write to the coupling facility, getting feedback as to whether the structure is under stress. If the GBP is indeed under stress, DB2 can write certain types of pages to DASD instead of waiting to write them to the group buffer pool. The types of pages that qualify for group buffer pool write-around are pages that aren't already in the group buffer pool and are also being written asynchronously after hitting a local buffer pool threshold, or after a system checkpoint. Synchronous writes caused by force-at-commit must still be written to the group buffer pool.

Another change, in the area of castout, is reducing the wait time for I/O completion by trying to overlap reads from the group buffer pool for castout with writing the pages to DASD. Moreover, DB2 11 reduces the size of the messages sent from the castout structure owner to the castout data set owner by sending the object IDs to be cast out instead of all individual page IDs. And, just as for local buffer pools, you can now provide a more granular specification for the CLASST castout threshold, specifying the number of pages for this value.

DB2's use of the coupling facility's DELETE_NAME operation is also enhanced with two new DELETE_NAME options. Starting with DB2 Version 6, DB2 used DELETE_NAME to purge pages from the coupling facility cache structure when an object was going out of group buffer pool dependency.

The first of the new options improves the efficiency of DELETE_NAME, especially where a customer has a geographically extended data sharing group, by suppressing cross invalidation (XI) signals. For those who are not yet planning to move to DB2 11, this enhancement was retrofitted back to DB2 10 and DB2 9 via APAR PM67544.

The second new option provides a safety net to detect unexpected errors—for example, cases where DB2 tries to use DELETE_NAME to purge pages from the group buffer pool when there are still some remaining pages left in the structure that must be written out to DASD.

Moving on, a new option value, CASTOUT, is provided for Restart Light. The command -START DB2 LIGHT(CASTOUT) causes all retained locks to be removed except for in-doubt or postponed abort units of recovery. This is accomplished by initiating CASTOUT at the end of Restart Light. Once CASTOUT processing is completed for a given object, the pageset can move out of group buffer pool dependency, and the retained pageset P-lock can be safely removed. Utilities and applications that previously would have been blocked by the pageset P-lock state can now be allowed to execute.

There is a very rare but troublesome case during group restart in which DB2 can place some indexes into rebuild-pending (RBDP) status, meaning you must run the REBUILD INDEX utility to clear the condition and make the index available. If, for example, the index is a large NPI for a very large partitioned table, this situation could lead to a significant DB2 application service outage. DB2 11 avoids this condition, and thus avoids any potential application service outage time.

One of the performance challenges in data sharing is when a GBP-dependent index suffers index leaf page splits, leading to performance problems. In a previous release of DB2, the number of force writes to the log was reduced from five to two. DB2 11 now takes this a step further by reducing the number of force writes to the log from two to one. Index split performance is also improved by reducing the number of force writes to the log for pseudo-delete cleanup. There is a very rare condition affecting index split performance when a rollback occurs. Before DB2 11, this process required up to five force writes to the log, but the process is now reduced to two force writes.

DB2 9 provided automatic group buffer pool recovery for any GRECP condition discovered at the end of DB2 restart. In DB2 11, this support is extended to automatic LPL recovery discovered at the end of DB2 restart. This enhancement simplifies operational procedures and makes applications available earlier after a failure.

The final data sharing improvement is for a special case, where only one member of a multi-member data sharing group has interest in an object, and that interest is read-only. Previously, if you opened a cursor that was defined as FOR UPDATE, DB2 would propagate the child U-lock to the coupling facility. Now, DB2 delays propagation of the child U-lock to the coupling facility until it has detected inter-system read-write interest at the level of the parent pageset P-lock.

Security Enhancements

In DB2 11, the synergy between DB2 and IBM Resource Access Control Facility (RACF®) is improved in a number of ways. The first of these causes cached DB2 authorizations and static SQL packages to be invalidated when RACF changes are made. New ZPARM AUTHEXT_CACHEREFRESH is used to activate the new behavior. Second, in the event of an AUTOBIND, BIND, or REBIND operation, DB2 will pass the accessor environment element (ACEE) of the package owner to RACF.

Another new ZPARM, AUTHEXIT_CHECK, is used for dynamic SQL authorization checking. When the DYNAMICRULES bind parameter is not set to RUN, DB2 presents the appropriate AUTHID to RACF, depending on the DYNAMICRULES setting. The AUTHID could therefore belong to the package owner, the ID that defined the routine, or the ID invoking the routine.

Beyond the improvements in the area of synergy with RACF, a new option for the BIND PLAN command, PROGAUTH, can be used to request program authorization checking to ensure a particular program and plan combination is authorized. Last, some of DB2 10's column-masking restrictions for queries with GROUP BY and DISTINCT have been removed.

Utility Enhancements

DB2 11 is probably the biggest release in terms of utility enhancements. There are so many enhancements that we summarize them here without going into many details:

- With each DB2 release, IBM has continually worked to reduce the outage for REORG, and DB2 11 is no exception. In DB2 11, drain processing is improved so that there is a better chance drain will be successful.

  o The elapsed time of the SWITCH phase has been reduced significantly. DB2 11 gives you more control over the timing of this phase by letting you specify when it should take place.

- Unless a partitioned table space has an auxiliary large object (LOB) table space, you can now specify SHRLEVEL CHANGE for REORG with REBALANCE.

- Processing for REORG and LOAD processing is now faster.

- The need to run RUNSTATS outside REORG is reduced because many more RUNSTATS options can be run as inline statistics, with the additional benefit of zIIP offload.

- Recovery from partition-level inline image copies is now faster, and if you use the &PA. or &PART. variable on your template, inline image copies for REORG are taken at the part level—even if you reorganize an entire partitioned table space. RECOVER can then use part-level image copies if recovery is required.

- Not only is more utility parallelism available, but more control over that parallelism is also provided.

  o In addition to utility performance improvements, DB2 11 simplifies data management and improves usability.

- REORG can automatically generating the mapping table and index and has more intelligent defaults.

- Partition-by-growth (PBG) management is improved by allowing REORG to shrink the number of partitions for UTS PBG. This behavior is controlled by a new ZPARM, REORG_DROP_PBG_PARTS, whose default setting is DISABLE.

- The Cross-loader now features improved XML handling. System cloning has been enhanced. And some of the point-in-time recovery restrictions associated with a materializing REORG of pending alters have been removed, so in these cases you'll be able to recover to a point in time before the materializing REORG.

- The DISPLAY UTILITY command provides better information about the status of utility execution, and, finally in this section, support for statistics profiles has been enhanced.

Analytics Improvements

In this section, we focus on the analytics improvements in DB2 11. These improvements include temporal data enhancements with support for views and special registers, transparent archive query, new analytics features, and integration with big data.

Temporal Data Enhancements

DB2 11 introduces support for a period specification when a view is referenced in a FROM clause by an SQL SELECT, UPDATE, or DELETE statement. A couple of examples illustrate how that works.

The first example is a SELECT against a view on a table with a system time specification, where the SELECT specifies a system time period:

```
CREATE VIEW v01 (col1, col2, col3) AS SELECT * FROM stt;

SELECT * FROM v01
    FOR SYSTEM_TIME AS OF TIMESTAMP '2010-01-10 10:00:00';
```

The second example references a similar sort of view, this time on a table with a business time specification; in this case, an UPDATE and a DELETE are issued against the view, specifying a portion of business time.

```
CREATE VIEW v8 (col1, col2, col3) AS SELECT * FROM att;

UPDATE v8
FOR PORTION OF BUSINESS_TIME FROM '2009-01-01' TO '2009-06-01'

SET c2 = c2 + 1.10;

DELETE FROM v8
    FOR PORTION OF BUSINESS_TIME FROM '2009-01-01' TO '2009-06-01'
    WHERE COL1 = 12345;
```

To enable you to retrieve data from temporal tables without modifying existing SQL, DB2 11 adds support for two temporal special registers, CURRENT TEMPORAL SYSTEM_TIME and CURRENT TEMPORAL BUSINESS_TIME. You can set these special registers to specify a system time or a business period and then execute existing SQL statements as if they had the system time or business period specified.

Two new BIND options, SYSTIMESENSITIVE and BUSTIMESENSITIVE, are used to enable use of the new temporal special registers. To allow the special registers to modify the execution of your queries, you must set one or both of the new BIND options to YES, depending on which special registers you want to use.

Transparent Archive Query

Transparent archive query is designed for the case where only a portion of your data is active or current and is possibly dynamic and subject to INSERT, UPDATE, and DELETE processing. The rest of the data is read-only historical data and is probably referenced infrequently. What you might want to do is to store this data in two tables. The first table would be the current data table, which you'd want to have on high-performance storage with high availability. The second would be a read-only history or archive table, which you could decide to move to more economical storage and possibly offload to the IBM DB2 Analytics Accelerator (IDAA).

Transparent archive query enables applications to query both the current and archive tables with no SQL changes. In other words, the fact that there are two tables is hidden from the application, which is presented with a single table image. By default, an SQL query on the data will retrieve data only from the current or base table. A new global variable, GET_ARCHIVE, can be set to allow the same query to retrieve data from both the base table and the archive table. If you set the special global variable, DB2 automatically converts the SQL to use UNION ALL to select from both tables using dynamic plan switching.

The archiving process of moving data from the current data table to the history table can be user-controlled. However, DB2 11 provides a new global variable, called MOVE_TO_ARCHIVE, that causes a deleted base table row to be moved to the archive table.

Both the base table and the history table have to be created by the user, and the structures of the two tables must be identical. They can be connected by using a new DDL clause, ALTER TABLE ENABLE ARCHIVE.

New Analytics Features

DB2 11 provides improved support for SQL grouping sets, including ROLLUP and CUBE. Previously, DB2 has had limited grouping set support; building each grouping set required a separate query. Now, ROLLUP and CUBE allow for multiple grouping sets inside the same SQL query. ROLLUP is helpful in providing subtotals along a hierarchical dimension, and CUBE is useful for queries that aggregate columns based on multiple dimensions.

Already noted is the performance enhancement for IFI filtering of IFCID 306, used by IDAA V3 with Change Data Capture. DB2 11 also provides this support for IDAA V4:

- DB2 changes can be propagated to the accelerator as they happen.

- The staleness of accelerator data can be detected via RTS.

- Disk storage cost can be reduced by archiving data in the accelerator using the High Performance Storage Saver, maintaining high performance for analytical queries.

- Workload Manager integration is improved, and better monitoring capabilities are provided.

- The query offload scope can be increased by using the new special register CURRENT QUERY ACCELERATION.

- High-performance IBM SPSS® in-database scoring via the PACK and UNPACK functions is available in DB2 11. This improvement has been retrofitted to DB2 10 via APAR.

Integration with Big Data

There is no doubt that there is huge interest industry-wide in big data. DB2 11 delivers support for integration with big data by providing connectors to allow DB2 applications to access data stored in Hadoop (a distributed file system) easily and efficiently. This is done by providing new user-defined functions (UDFs) and a new generic table UDF capability.

The goal in this support is to integrate DB2 for z/OS with the Hadoop-based IBM BigInsights™ platform, enabling traditional applications on DB2 for z/OS to access big data analytics. Analytics jobs can be specified using the JavaScript Object Notation (JSON) query language known as Jaql and submitted to IBM InfoSphere BigInsights. The results are then stored in the Hadoop Distributed File System (HDFS), and a table UDF, HDFS_READ, reads the result from the HDFS for subsequent presentation to an SQL query.

New Application Features

Continuing the theme of application enablement, DB2 11 includes a number of very welcome new application features.

Global variables allow application developers to have named global variables, stored in memory. The variables can be accessed and modified via SQL and can be shared across multiple SQL statements within the same database connection.

The SQL Procedural Language (SQL PL) has been improved in terms of performance, manageability, and function, with two significant enhancements. The first improvement is autonomous transactions, which lets a called stored procedure commit as if it were a separate business transaction. This improvement might prove useful, for example, if a stored procedure is called to record all data access attempts and needs to commit regardless of whether the calling transaction is completed successfully or is aborted. Second, SQL PL adds support for the array data type, which can be used in stored procedures and user-defined function. The array data type can be passed in as an argument or a result of a UDF or as IN, OUT, or INOUT parameters for a stored procedure.

DB2 11 provides alias support for sequence objects, in two forms. As with tables and views, you can define a private alias. Introduced in DB2 11, you can also define a public alias, with the implicit qualifier SYSPUBLIC. The public alias feature is available only for sequences.

Mobile Application Support

Both DB2 10 and DB2 11 support the JSON API, which is widely used for mobile applications. Now, DB2 for z/OS for mobile-style applications can use a common API, letting both SQL and JSON be issued from a single application.

Easier DB2 Version Upgrade with Application SQL Compatibility

Our last topic is a very significant one. IBM developers heard loudly and clearly the complaints from customers, particularly over recent releases, concerning the number of incompatible SQL changes, the late documentation of these changes, and the difficulty in implementing the changes. New DB2 releases can introduce changes to SQL behavior that break existing applications. Some of these changes have arisen out of the need to fix a defect. Rather than introduce the change as a fix in the service stream, IBM has chosen to introduce the change on a release boundary. Other changes have been introduced because of changes to the SQL standard.

Regardless of the reason for these changes, the lateness of the documentation updates and the large number of changes to be investigated made it difficult for customers to identify and resolve all SQL incompatibility issues before migrating to a new release. In any event, many customers indicated that they wanted to be able to make the necessary changes application by application, package by package, in a phased approach.

To address these issues, DB2 11 provides a new mechanism to enable customers to identify applications affected by the SQL changes and change those applications at the individual package level. Customers who prefer to do so can still introduce changed behavior at the system level; however, the expectation is that most customers will make these changes application by application, at the package level.

The new function does not avoid the need to make the application changes. These changes must happen at some point. However, the key point is that IBM has now separated out the process of making application changes from system release migration, meaning customers can introduce the changes in a piecemeal fashion, during the lifetime of the new release.

In fact, the new mechanism provides support for up to two back-level releases. So, for example, when you migrate to DB2 11, some of your SQL statements might well be incompatible with the new release, but you will be able to investigate and resolve these incompatibility issues during the life of DB2 11 or the life of the next DB2 release.

For customers still on DB2 9, DB2 11 will not support incompatible SQL semantics and behavior from DB2 9. DB2 10 is the lowest level of application compatibility supported by the new feature.

To implement the new function, DB2 11 provides a new BIND option, APPLCOMPAT. When in DB2 11 conversion mode, the only application-level support is for DB2 10, so APPLCOMPAT(V10R1) is forced. All existing packages are tagged in the catalog on entry to DB2 11 CM with the application compatibility level of V10R1. Once the ENFM process has been completed and you have entered new-function mode, you can then bind your applications, using BIND ADD or BIND REPLACE, with an application compatibility level of V11R1, or you can continue to specify V10R1. Note that specifying APPLCOMPAT(V11R1) indicates that all SQL in the package is compatible with DB2 11 and that you have eliminated any incompatibilities.

It is also the case that you need to use APPLCOMPAT(V11R1) to use any of the new SQL features introduced in DB2 11. But if you haven't resolved all SQL incompatibilities, you can continue to use BIND ADD and BIND REPLACE with APPLCOMPAT(V10R1).

If you incur SQL problems when your packages are still bound with option APPLCOMPAT(V10R1), IBM provides support to enable those packages to continue to behave as if you were in DB2 10. Note, by the way, that this support does not apply to access path changes.

DB2 11 for z/OS: Migration Planning and Early Customer Experiences

by John Campbell and Gareth Jones

IBM® DB2® 11 for IBM z/OS® is the 15th release of the enterprise relational database management system (RDBMS) of choice. The purpose of this white paper is not only to help customers move to the new release smoothly, safely, and quickly but also to exploit significant enhancements: performance and scalability improvements, including CPU savings; enhanced resiliency and continuous availability; and the many enhancements to the DB2 utilities.

Customers on the DB2 11 for z/OS Early Support Program (ESP) tested DB2 10 to DB2 11 migration and DB2 11 enhancements and new features. Their experiences provide a solid foundation for the following objectives:

- Share lessons learned

- Provide migration hints, tips, and additional planning information

- Provide usage guidelines and positioning on new enhancements

- Help customers to migrate as fast as possible, without compromising safety

Customer experiences, test results, and feedback have enabled the publication of this white paper. To help customers structure their plans to migrate to DB2 11 effectively, this document is composed of the following sections:

- Major themes of DB2 11

- ESP highlights

- Migration considerations

- Availability

- Utilities

- Performance and scalability

DB2 11 Major Themes

Before commencing migration to DB2 11, customers first need to be satisfied that doing so will provide benefits in terms of resilience, availability, scalability, performance, and cost effectiveness. Four major DB2 11 themes address these requirements: CPU savings, enhanced resiliency and continuous availability, enhanced business analytics, and simpler, faster DB2 version upgrades.

CPU Savings

The DB2 11 theme that has attracted the most attention is the potential to realize CPU savings without the need for application changes, as this has the potential to reduce running costs across the entire IBM System z® software stack for Monthly License Charge (MLC) customers. Although there is no need for application changes to exploit DB2 11 to reduce CPU costs, in most cases a REBIND is required for static SQL plans. The following are CPU savings customers can expect:

- 0 to 10 percent for OLTP

- 0 to 10 percent for update-intensive batch

- 0 to 40 percent for queries

- Additional performance improvements through use of new DB2 11 features

Further information about DB2 11 CPU savings is available in other IBM white papers, IBM Redbooks®, and DB2 11 for z/OS product documentation.

Enhanced Resiliency and Continuous Availability

DB2 for z/OS has been the high-availability RDBMS market leader for many years, and significant DB2 11 resilience and availability improvements ensure that this lead is maintained or even extended. This is important for the DB2 for z/OS customer base because businesses continually demand improvements in the areas of continuous availability and resilience, so that they can deliver a better service to their customers. To help customers minimize the impact of IT incidents, and to eliminate or minimize the impact of application changes, database schema changes, database maintenance, and software changes, DB2 11 introduces a number of improvements:

- Improved autonomics to reduce costs and improve availability

- The ability to make more online changes without affecting application availability

- Online REORG improvements, meaning less disruption

- Two new capabilities: DROP COLUMN and the online change of partition limit keys

- Extension of the DB2 log capacity to 1 yottabyte (YB), or 1 billion petabytes (PB), meaning that the DB2 can run for thousands of years before customers have to reset the log

- Allowing BIND/REBIND, DDL, and some kinds of online REORG operations to break into persistent threads (this affects online REORG utilities that materialize pending schema changes)

Enhanced Business Analytics

As customers seek to exploit the vast and rapidly increasing amount of data stored in their critical business applications, DB2 11 introduces a range of enhanced business analytics capabilities to help turn that data into valuable information:

- Expanded SQL, XML, and analytics capabilities

- Temporal table enhancements

- Transparent archiving—the ability to automatically insert rows deleted from a base table into an archive table

- SQL PL enhancements, including support for the array data type

- Hadoop integration

- NoSQL and JSON support

Simpler, Faster DB2 Version Upgrades

The number and complexity of DB2 enhancements have resulted in significant changes to the DB2 catalog and directory. This means that migration to new releases has often been complicated and disruptive and has required careful planning. With each new release, the DB2 for z/OS development team has tried to make migration easier, faster, and safer, and they have continued to do so with DB2 11. This requirement has been addressed in a number of ways:

- Improved product quality and reliability, achieved via an iterative approach to development: a series of three-month cycles composed of 1:N rallies leading to functional verification testing (FVT), system verification test (SVT), performance test, and finally a stabilization phase ahead of the start of the Early Support Program

- Separating application changes from the DB2 system upgrade via the new APPLCOMPAT feature

- Improvements in ensuring access path stability after REBIND

ESP Highlights

The DB2 11 Early Support Program, managed by IBM BetaWorks, started in February 2013 with 21 worldwide customers:

- Eleven in EMEA
- Nine in North America
- One in South America

In terms of industry sector, the breakdown was as follows:

- Seven in banking
- Five in insurance
- Three in healthcare
- Two in financial markets
- One in the automotive sector

After education workshops in Germany and the United States, the first code drop was in March 2013. In July 2013, the "regular" service process of maintenance being delivered via PTF and APAR fix commenced. The ESP then entered another phase, with an extra six worldwide customers joining:

- Three in EMEA
- Two in North America
- One in South America

The industry breakdown was as follows:

- Three in banking
- Two in computer services
- One in professional services

Following a highly successful ESP, DB2 11 for z/OS was announced on October 1, 2013, and the product became generally available (GA) on October 25, 2013.

DB2 11 Early Support Program Customer Feedback

The ESP customers reported that product quality was excellent at this early stage in the release cycle, and that reliability was also very impressive compared with previous releases. The performance improvements were good, with CPU savings for different workload types as follows:

- DRDA workload up to 20 percent CPU reduction
- CICS workload up to 18 percent CPU reduction

- Batch workload up to 20 percent CPU reduction

Although the range of features that were tested inevitably varied from customer to customer, some common themes emerged.

BIND, REBIND, DDL, and Online REORG Break-in

DB2 11 makes it much easier for operations that bind packages or make database schema changes to break in alongside an active workload, even with persistent threads (e.g., protected CICS entry threads or IMS Pseudo Wait For Input, or WFI). If an operation needs to invalidate or quiesce a package held by a RELEASE(DEALLOCATE) thread, this popular improvement implicitly releases that package, making it much easier for the operation to obtain the package locks needed to complete successfully. BIND and REBIND commands, DDL changes, and online REORG used to materialize a pending definition change (often referred to as "deferred ALTER") all benefit from this enhancement.

Transparent Archiving

Many customers need to retain historical or inactive data for longer and longer periods of time, whether for regulatory compliance, data analysis or other reasons. This typically leads to a significant increase in the amount of stored data, which can impact response times and the ability to meet service level agreements (SLAs) and make it more difficult to manage and schedule database housekeeping operations. Transparent archiving offers a solution by enabling applications to use the same SQL to access a base table, with or without its associated archive table, depending on the setting of a built-in global variable. Another global variable enables customers to specify whether the archive table is automatically populated by DB2. This is done by transparently moving rows deleted from the base table to the archive table. As an alternative, customers can implement their own set of processes and procedures for archiving data.

IFI 306 Filtering by Object

Applications, such as Q Replication (QREP) Capture, that read the DB2 log to replicate data updates can take advantage of IFI filtering to ensure that DB2 presents log records only for the objects being replicated. This feature can improve performance and save CPU, especially where a small subset of the objects is replicated.

Online Schema Change

DB2 10 introduced the ability to make several types of changes to objects (indexes and table spaces) while applications are still running, such as segment size, page size, and the MEMBER CLUSTER attribute. DB2 11 adds the ability to alter partition limit keys and, more significantly, the ability in some cases to recover to a point-in-time prior to a successful materializing REORG.

Utility Improvements

DB2 11 is the most effective release of DB2 in terms of utility improvements, including online REORG enhancements and improved usability, availability, and performance.

Extended RBA/LSRN

In releases prior to DB2 11, the 6-byte log record relative byte address (RBA) has provided 256 TB of log record addressing capacity over the life of a non-data sharing DB2 subsystem or member of a DB2 data sharing group. There is a process for handling the situation where the addressing capacity is exhausted—resetting the log—but this method is highly disruptive, especially for a non-data sharing subsystem. Data sharing users are affected not only by the log RBA constraints, but in some cases they can also wrap the log record sequence number (LRSN). Normally, the LRSN should provide enough capacity to last until 2042. However, if a LRSN delta is needed (for example, where data sharing has been disabled and then re-enabled), the LRSN can be "in the future," meaning it will wrap much sooner.

DB2 11 solves this potential issue by expanding the RBA and LRSN to 10 bytes, delivering much greater log capacity: up to 1 YB in terms of the RBA and up to 30,000 years in terms of the LRSN. In addition, the extended LRSN improves LRSN granularity, effectively eliminating the possibility of spinning on the processor to wait for the LRSN to be incremented.

Once in new-function mode (NFM), customers can determine whether they need to convert to the extended RBA/LRSN, decide on the timing of the conversion, and perform the conversion in piecemeal fashion, object by object.

Other Popular Improvements

Other enhancements that proved popular with the ESP customers include DB2 optimizer and migration improvements and GROUP BY grouping sets.

Migration Considerations

The key to a successful DB2 11 migration project is careful planning and preparation. This section provides advice and guidance to help with your planning.

Prerequisites: Hardware and Software

One of the first items in your DB2 11 migration plan should be to make sure that you meet the hardware and software requirements.

Customer Quotes
from the DB2 11 Early Support Program

"Overall we are very satisfied and astonished about the system stability of DB2 V11. In V10 we experienced this in another way."—*European Insurance*

"We have seen very few problems in [installation, migration, and performance]. Overall, it has been a very pleasant experience!! . . . The quality of the code is clearly much higher than for the ESP for DB2 10. . . . "
—European Banking/FSS

"Good code stability, no outages, no main failures, only a few PMRs. . . . "
—European Banking/FSS

"We have been involved in several DB2 for z/OS ESPs. This one will rank as one of, if not the smoothest one yet."   —*Large NA Retailer*

"I saw a significant performance improvement in recovery of catalog and directory (V10 5:53 minutes, V11 2:50 minutes). That rocks! . . . DB2 11 is the best version I have ever seen."   —*European Government*

"Overall, we have been impressed with the new version of DB2."
—NA Manufacturer

"Higher availability, performance, and lower CPU consumption, amongst other new features, were the benefits perceived by Banco do Brazil with DB2 11 for z/OS. During our testing with DB2 11, we noticed improved performance, along with stability."
—Paulo Sahadi, IT Executive, Banco do Brasil

"We have seen some incredible performance results with DB2 11, a major reduction of CPU time, 3.5% before REBIND and nearly 5% after REBIND. This will significantly bring down our operating costs."
—Conrad Wolf, Golden Living

Hardware Requirements

DB2 11 runs only on IBM zEnterprise® EC12 (zEC12), z196 and z10 processors supporting z/Architecture. You should also plan for increased real storage requirements compared to DB2 10 for z/OS (typically up to 15 percent).

One way to estimate the real storage requirement is to use the information supplied in IFCID 225 to calculate the total real storage used by DB2 10. Next, subtract the total size of the virtual buffer pools, and add an extra 15 percent to be more cautious to the remainder. Add back in the size of the virtual buffer pools, and the result provides an estimate of the real storage requirements for DB2 11.

Software Requirements

The software requirements for DB2 11 are mainly, but not exclusively, at the OS level:

- z/OS V1.13 Base Services (5694-A01) or higher

- DFSMS V1R13—the DB2 catalog is SMS-managed

- Language Environment Base Services

- z/OS Version 1 Release 13 Security Server (RACF)

- IRLM Version 2 Release 3 (shipped with DB2 11 for z/OS)

- z/OS Unicode Services and appropriate conversion definitions are required

- IBM DB2 Connect™ 10.5 Fixpack 2

- IBM InfoSphere® Data Replication (IIDR) 10.2.1 to support the extended LRSN in new-function mode

Prerequisites: DB2 Connect

For many customers, management of their DB2 Connect estate has been a cause for concern when migrating from one DB2 for z/OS release to another. This is typically the case where there are many workstations running a variety of DB2 Connect releases, which are not centrally managed. It can be very difficult, if not impossible, to ensure that the DB2 Connect level on all known workstations is updated to a supported release, and equally difficult to perform effective testing. This task becomes even harder when it is not possible to identify all the workstations that can connect to DB2.

DB2 11 cannot solve all these problems, but this paper provides an opportunity to outline what support is provided for DB2 Connect customers running with older, out-of-support product releases and to provide a brief summary of current recommended best practice.

DB2 11 for z/OS in all modes—conversion mode (CM), enabling-new-function mode (ENFM), and new-function mode—should operate with existing versions of DB2 Connect, even back to DB2 Connect Version 8. DB2 for z/OS Development will investigate any connectivity-related issues with existing applications that run on older versions of DB2 Connect and will try to provide a fix. If there are issues that cannot be resolved with a fix or other change in the DB2 for z/OS server itself, DB2 Connect will have to be upgraded to an in-service level to obtain a DB2 Connect fix.

For continuous availability during the migration process, the minimum recommended level of DB2 Connect operating with DB2 10 for z/OS is V9.7 FP6 or V10.1 FP2. This level provides continuous availability to the application server when DB2 for z/OS is migrated from DB2 10 NFM to DB2 11 CM, and on through DB2 11 ENFM to DB2 11 NFM.

The minimum level for full DB2 11 for z/OS exploitation is currently V10.5 FP2. This level is required for specific new functions, including support for using arrays as input and output variables with stored procedures, workload balancing and automatic client reroute support with global variables, auto-commit performance improvements, and improved client information. As customer adoption of DB2 11 broadens, it is likely that the recommended level will be set higher, with fixes for defects being included in new driver levels and with documented best practice being updated with the new DB2 Connect and data server driver release and fix-pack levels.

While it remains the case that most DB2 for z/OS engine features in NFM are supported with any version of DB2 Connect, DB2 for z/OS Development is being proactive in recommending that customers move from the DB2 Connect client or runtime client packages to using the data server (ds) driver instead.

There are many customers who periodically update their DB2 Connect release and fix-pack levels because they want to ensure that they are always running on supported versions, even if the application doesn't change. For these customers, and for those who plan to exploit new function, the recommended order of upgrade for maximum stability and availability is the following:

- The DB2 for z/OS server.

- Any DB2 Connect servers, if present, but customers are encouraged to move to direct connect using the data server driver.

- Drivers installed directly on application servers. If you are using the DB2 Connect client or runtime client, it is recommended that you convert to using the data server driver instead.

- User workstations. Again, it is recommended that you convert from using the DB2 Connect client or runtime client to using the data server driver.

DB2 for z/OS Development does recognize that there are, however, customers who push out the drivers first. These are generally driven by the need for specific application enhancements, the most common example being in the .NET arena where customers want the latest tooling and driver support for applications and application servers running on Microsoft® platforms.

Pre-Migration Planning

It is important to identify what work needs to be done to prepare your DB2 10 subsystems and data sharing groups for migration to DB2 11. DB2 provides tooling to help you do this, in the form of the pre-migration job, DSNTIJPM.

DSNTIJPM ships with DB2 11 and should be run on DB2 10 to identify any pre-migration catalog cleanup requirements. The same job is shipped for DB2 10 via APAR PM94057 in the form of job DSNTIJPB to maximize the available time for you to prepare to migrate.

In either case, make sure you have applied APAR PI11236 before running the pre-migration job. Run DSNTIJPM or DSNTIJPB, read the various reports produced to check for situations needing attention before migration, and take the actions recommended by the report headers. DSNTIJPM/DSNTIJPB may provide extra assistance in the form of DDL or utility statements for any required cleanup jobs.

Important Preparation

There are some important steps you should take in DB2 10 before starting migration. Any old plans and packages that were rebound prior to DB2 V9.1 or before should be rebound. Otherwise, they will be automatically rebound by DB2 11 on first use, preventing you from exercising control over access path selection.

Any views, materialized query tables (MQTs), or table functions with a period specification created in DB2 10 should be dropped, as they are no longer supported in DB2 11. A period specification is valid only if specified on a base table.

Items Deprecated in Earlier Versions, Now Eliminated

Identify whether you are using any features that were deprecated in earlier releases of DB2 and have now been eliminated:

- Password protection for active log and archive log data sets is no longer supported; remove password protection before migrating to DB2 11.

- The DSNH CLIST no longer supports values of V8 or V9 for the NEWFUN parameter; use V10 or V11 instead. Update your DSNH procedures when you migrate from DB2 10 NFM to DB2 11 CM.

- Some DB2-supplied routines are no longer supported:

  o The Explain stored procedure, SYSPROC.DSNAEXP, is obsolete; use the EXPLAIN privilege and issue EXPLAIN directly.

  o The MQ Application Messaging Interface (AMI) DB2 MQ (DB2MQ) being injected into the system functions in schemas

DB2MQ1C, DB2MQ2C, DB2MQ1N, and DB2MQ2N are now obsolete; use the MQI-based functions in schemas DMQXML1C and DMQXML2C instead (see APAR PK37290 for further guidance). You should make these changes before migrating to DB2 11.

- The DSNHDECP application programming default parameter CHARSET is no longer supported. This parameter was used to specify whether the character set associated with the default EBCDIC CCSID was ALPHANUM or KATAKANA; it was used by the DB2 parser prior to DB2 V8.1. However, from DB2 V8.1 onward, statements are parsed in Unicode instead of EBCDIC, and the parser therefore no longer needs to know whether the character set is alphanumeric or Katakana. Before assembling DSNHDECP at DB2 11, make sure this parameter is not specified in the DSNHDECP source deck.

- The BIND PACKAGE ENABLE and DISABLE (REMOTE) options no longer support the REMOTE sub-option with a list of location names or LU names—specific names cannot be specified. Alter your BIND and REBIND procedures to make sure the REMOTE sub-option is no longer used. Be aware that ENABLE(REMOTE) and DISABLE(REMOTE) will enable or disable all remote connections for the affected package.

- Support for Sysplex query parallelism is removed. Single-member parallelism is still supported, and any packages that used Sysplex query parallelism prior to DB2 11 will use CPU parallelism in DB2 11.

- The DSN1CHKR utility is no longer available, as there are no links in the catalog or directory. You should therefore remove DSN1CHKR from your catalog and directory maintenance procedures.

Preparing Your Current DB2 10 NFM for Migration to DB2 11 CM

To prepare your DB2 10 new-function mode systems for migration to DB2 11, there are some further steps you must take. To begin migration, your DB2 10 subsystem must be at the proper service level. The starting point is to apply the fallback SPE APAR, PM31841, and any prerequisite fixes. Info APAR II14660 details any further service recommendations, but early on in the lifecycle of DB2 11, it is strongly recommended that you are vigilant on maintenance, paying special attention to HIPER and PE APARs.

If you are non-data sharing, the only requirement is that your DB2 10 NFM system must have been started with the SPE APAR PM31841 applied; otherwise, DB2 11 will terminate when you start it, and you will be unable to progress to DB2 11 CM until you have restarted your DB2 10 system with the correct maintenance.

If you are data sharing, before migrating the first member to DB2 11, all other started DB2 10 members must have the fallback SPE APAR applied for DB2 11 to start. If there are any active members without the SPE applied, DB2 11 will terminate. The recommended practice is to restart all data sharing members with the SPE applied before commencing migration, even if you plan to have a single member active when you start DB2 11 for the first time.

You should also ensure that there are no entries in SYSUTILX prior to starting DB2 11 for the first time, and prior to entering enabling-new-function mode; otherwise CATMAINT and ENFM will not execute because DB2 11 no longer blindly re-initializes SYSUTILX. This means all utility processing must be cleaned up before shutting down DB2 10.

You should run standard online REORGs against the catalog and directory objects before commencing ENFM/NFM migration, preferably as part of a different change slot. The objective is to check that REORG can break in, to check the data consistency of catalog and directory, and to improve the performance of the ENFM process.

DB2 11 Migration Overview

Figure 2.1 illustrates the DB2 11 migration process.

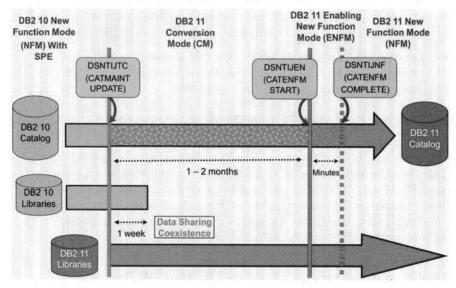

Figure 2.1: DB2 11 migration process

Once you have started and stopped DB2 10 with the SPE applied, you can start DB2 11 for the first time. Once restart has completed, run the CATMAINT

UPDATE job, DSNTIJTC. This takes you into DB2 11 conversion mode. If you are data sharing, you enter a state called "data sharing coexistence" until you have started all data sharing members with the DB2 11 libraries. It is strongly recommended that you minimize the time in data sharing coexistence to avoid side effects such as different access paths being chosen on different members.

Once you are confident that you will not fall back to DB2 10, you can then enter ENFM, by running the CATENFM START job, DSNTIJEN, and enter NFM by running the CATENFM COMPLETE job, DSNTIJNF. Once this last job is completed, your catalog will have been fully converted to a DB2 11 catalog.

Migration and Fallback Paths

DB2 11 always enables you to drop back to the previous stage of the migration process. However, you cannot fall back to DB2 10 NFM after entry to DB2 11 ENFM, but you can return to DB2 11 CM*. The star (*) indicates that at some point you entered a later phase of the migration process but decided to fall back. Note that, as Figure 2.2 illustrates, you can fall back from NFM to either CM* or ENFM*. The numbers by the arrows refer to the jobs you have to run when you move from one phase or mode to another.

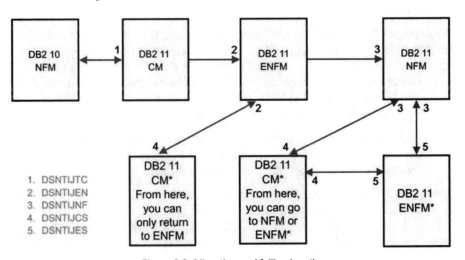

Figure 2.2: Migration and fallback paths

APPLCOMPAT: Application Compatibility

Customers have typically faced a significant challenge when preparing to migrate to a new DB2 release: dealing with any SQL incompatibilities introduced by the new release that need to be addressed before migration. To provide a solution to this problem, the requirements must first be defined.

The Requirements

Eliminating the need to deal with incompatible SQL Data Manipulation Language (DML) and XML by making application changes during migration requires that the process of changing application programs be decoupled from the system migration to the new DB2 release that introduced the incompatible SQL DML and XML changes.

To be useful to customers, any solution should provide a mechanism to identify application programs affected by incompatible SQL DML and XML changes, and it should also provide a mechanism to introduce changes at an individual application program (package) level. This means enabling support for phasing in application program changes over a much longer time, providing support for mixed DB2 release coexistence in data sharing, and enabling support for up to two back-level releases of DB2 (*N–2*).

The Solution

In DB2 11 a new ZPARM, APPLCOMPAT, delivers on those requirements. It separates DB2 system migration to the new DB2 release from application program migration to deal with incompatible SQL DML and XML introduced by the new release.

The APPLCOMPAT ZPARM specifies the default value for the new BIND and REBIND APPLCOMPAT option. Because this is the first release of DB2 to support APPLCOMPAT, there are only two valid values, both for the ZPARM and for the BIND/REBIND option: V10R1 for DB2 10 SQL DML and XML behavior, and V11R1 for DB2 11 SQL DML and XML behavior. The default ZPARM setting is V11R1 for new installs and is V10R1 for migration.

Customers can use the APPLCOMPAT BIND/REBIND option to override the default value specified by the ZPARM; for dynamic SQL the CURRENT APPLICATION COMPATIBILITY special register performs the same function.

You should be aware of the limitations of APPLCOMPAT. It does not address issues with new reserved words or other incompatibilities that could only be resolved by having multiple levels of the DB2 parser, and the BIF_COMPATIBILITY ZPARM introduced in DB2 10 is independent of APPLCOMPAT.

Because APPLCOMPAT affects behavior at the application program level, new SQL functionality available in DB2 11 NFM cannot be used until the relevant package is bound with an APPLCOMPAT value of V11R1.

When migrating from DB2 10 NFM, APPLCOMPAT is automatically set to V10R1 before NFM. If you try to override this setting with BIND or REBIND, DB2 will cause the operation to fail, returning an error message:

```
DSNT225I -DSN BIND ERROR FOR PACKAGE location.collid.member
APPLCOMPAT(V11R1) OPTION IS NOT SUPPORTED
```

DB2 11 delivers new instrumentation to identify where DB2 10–specific functionality is used, via IFCID 376. IFCID 376 provides a summary of DB2 10 function usage, and IFCID 366 provides detailed information, identifying the packages involved. It is expected that changes necessary to avoid V10R1 usage will be made only after reaching NFM.

One way to start converting applications to be tagged with V11R1 is to rebind those applications that don't have a dependency on DB2 10–specific functionality first and then move on to convert those applications that are dependent. A workaround to distinguish packages that have to run as V10R1 until they are corrected is to annotate the package using

```
SQL COMMENT ON PACKAGE colid.name."version" IS 'V10R1'
```

If *version* is a precompiler timestamp, then the double quotes (") are necessary. This information is stored in the REMARKS column of the SYSIBM.SYSPACKAGE table and can be queried and exploited by housekeeping to ensure that APPLCOMPAT(V10R1) is used for these packages until they are converted and the comment is removed or updated.

Availability

A significant factor influencing customers to migrate to DB2 11 is the opportunity to improve application availability, and there are a number of areas where customers need to plan to exploit this opportunities.

BIND/REBIND/DDL/Online REORG Break-in with Persistent RELEASE(DEALLOCATE) Threads

Making use of persistent threads running packages that are bound with RELEASE(DEALLOCATE)—such as IMS Pseudo WFI regions and CICS protected entry threads—can potentially provide very significant performance benefits. Prior to DB2 11, they can block processes such as BIND, REBIND, and DDL scripts and can also block two types of the online REORG utility, REORG REBALANCE and a materializing REORG, which invalidate packages.

DB2 11 addresses this with a new form of behavior, which is on by default but can be controlled by ZPARM PKGREL_COMMIT. It enables BIND, REBIND, DDL, and online REORG to "break in" to persistent threads running packages bound with RELEASE(DEALLOCATE) and complete successfully. Break-in is not guaranteed and is performed on a best-efforts basis. It can handle idling threads that are at a transaction boundary; that is, where commit or abort was the last thing performed.

Several factors determine whether break-in is successful or not. The persistent thread must COMMIT for the mechanism to work, and the timing and frequency of COMMIT are both key in allowing break-in. To improve the chances of a successful break-in, consider increasing the ZPARM for the IRLM resource timeout interval (IRLMRWT).

The break-in mechanism does not apply when you are running packages bound with KEEPDYNAMIC(YES), when you have open WITH HOLD cursors defined WITH HOLD at the time of COMMIT, or if the COMMIT happens inside a stored procedure. However, operations such as BIND, REBIND, DDL, and some types of online REORG would not be able to break in under these conditions, even with threads running packages bound with RELEASE(COMMIT).

To be able to best exploit the break-in mechanism, it's important to understand how it works, step by step.

Step 1

When BIND, REBIND, DDL, or online REORG is initiated, it can wait for up to three times the IRLM timeout limit (IRLMRWT) for a package lock, after which the process will time out.

Step 2

At half of the IRLM timeout limit, IRLM will notify DB2 that a process is stuck waiting for a package lock. If the holder of the lock has an S-lock, DB2 will post a system task to take further action.

Step 3

The DB2 system task is awakened and checks to see whether a "recycle" of threads has been done in the past 10 seconds; the following steps describe the recycle process.

If no recycle has been done, the break-in operation will proceed. The reason for the 10-second threshold is that DB2 is trying to avoid flooding the system with recycle requests during BIND/REBIND/DDL/online REORG activity.

Step 4

In data sharing, the member where BIND, REBIND, DDL, or online REORG is running sends a broadcast to all the other members in the DB2 data sharing group to perform a recycle of locally attached threads.

Step 5

At this stage, the task loops through all locally attached threads (not distributed ones) to see whether the time since they last issued commit or abort was more than half that of the IRLM timeout limit (IRLMRWT). If so, chances are that the BIND/REBIND/DDL/online REORG is waiting on them.

Step 6

Next, DB2 tests to see whether it can do anything to release the package locks. To pass this test, each thread must be at a transaction boundary; that is, commit or abort was the last DB2 operation carried out. If so, DB2 can process the thread recycle request.

Step 7

DB2 "fences" the API for the thread to ensure the applications do not drive any new DB2 requests, takes control of the agent structure, and drives a "dummy COMMIT." The commit is safe because the thread is already at a transaction boundary. DB2 acts as the coordinator because this is a single-phase commit, and it releases the agent structure. On the COMMIT, RDS can see that there is a waiter for a package lock held by this agent and switches behavior to RELEASE(COMMIT) for this commit cycle. The package lock is then freed, taking the BIND/REBIND/DDL/online REORG one step closer to breaking in.

Step 8

DB2 repeats this process for all qualifying threads.

Step 9

BIND/REBIND/DDL/online REORG should break in, provided that there are no blocking threads holding the package lock that could not be recycled; for example, a long-running read-only application process without any intermediate commits.

Step 10

If the application starts using the thread during the recycle processing, it is blocked at the API level. DB2 causes the thread to spin in a timer-based wait loop until the recycle is complete—DB2 waits approximately a millisecond between polls to see whether the thread is available to the application. To protect the recycle process, DB2 also fences end-of-task conditions such as cancelling an application TCB or end-of-memory conditions such as forcing down the home ASID, for the duration of the recycle.

Persistent Thread Break-in: ESP Customer Testing Experiences

Customers on the DB2 11 Early Support Program tested persistent thread break-in for BIND, REBIND, DDL, and online REORG extensively. Table 2.1 summarizes the results of that testing.

Table 2.1: Test results – DB2 11 ESP persistent thread break-in		
Action	**Thread type**	**Results**
BIND	Batch, no Commit	No break-in
BIND	Batch, frequent Commit	Break-in
BIND	50* CICS ENTRY	Break-in
DDL	CICS ENTRY	Break-in
Create Index	CICS ENTRY	Break-in
Drop Index	CICS ENTRY	Break-in
Alter Table Add Column	CICS ENTRY	Break-in
Alter Index (NO) cluster	CICS ENTRY	Break-in
Alter Tablespace to UTS	CICS ENTRY	Break-in
Alter Partition	CICS ENTRY	Break-in

Improved Control When Altering Partition Limit Keys

Altering limit keys for partitioned table spaces can seriously impact availability, and the behavior differs depending on how the table partitioning is controlled.

With table-controlled table partitioning, alteration of limit keys is a pending ALTER, which is instantiated by a materializing REORG. Dropping of these alters can occur at any time before the REORG.

With index-controlled table partitioning, if the limit key change is done via ALTER INDEX ALTER PARTITION, the partition goes into a "hard" REORG-pending (REORP) state, and access to the partition is restricted until REORG is run, impacting availability. The table space remains index-controlled. In terms of control, the ALTER cannot be withdrawn once it has been issued.

Again with index-controlled table partitioning, if the alter is done by ALTER TABLE ALTER PARTITION, there are two possible behaviors. If the partition is not empty, then it goes into "hard" REORG-pending (REORP), and the table space is automatically converted to table-controlled partitioning. As before, the ALTER cannot be withdrawn after it has been issued. If, on the other hand, the partition is empty, the ALTER is executed immediately, and the table space is again converted to table-controlled partitioning. In either case, the conversion may be unwelcome.

DB2 11 doesn't change the behavior described above, but it introduces controls that can prevent changes that might affect availability from being injected into the system. Two new ZPARMs are introduced: PREVENT_ALTERTB_LIMITKEY and PREVENT_NEW_IXCTRL_PART.

PREVENT_ALTERTB_LIMITKEY causes any attempt to change partition limit keys using ALTER TABLE ALTER PARTITION to fail with SQLCODE –876. However, changing partition limit keys using ALTER INDEX ALTER PARTITION is still possible;

the recommendation is that you do not use this in production because of the impact of the REORP condition.

PREVENT_NEW_IXCTRL_PART stops you from creating new index-controlled partitioned table spaces, thereby ensuring you gain the availability benefits of table-controlled partitioning.

In addition to these benefits, a materializing REORG can now break in to a persistent thread running a package bound with RELEASE(DEALLOCATE).

REORG REBALANCE, in which DB2 alters the partition limit keys, can now be run with SHRLEVEL CHANGE. It can't be run for any partitions with pending ALTER LIMITKEY changes, but it will work for the other partitions and for partitions that are "hard" REORG-pending (REORP).

DROP COLUMN

DROP COLUMN has been a longstanding customer requirement, and it is introduced in DB2 11. ESP customers reported that this feature works well. You can convert to a universal table space (UTS) and concurrently DROP COLUMN in the same materializing REORG. The materializing REORG can be run at the partition level, but the table space remains in advisory REORG-pending status (AREOR) until all partitions have been reorganized. Note that all packages touching the table will be invalidated.

Some restrictions are associated with DROP COLUMN. It cannot be used against the classic table space type; DB2 will fail the SQL statement with SQLCODE –650. Any attempt to drop a column contained in an index or view will fail with SQLCODE –478. If you have a pending DROP COLUMN, you cannot add another column before the materializing REORG. You cannot create a view on a table with a pending dropped column. In both of these cases, DB2 will return SQLCODE –20385. If you try to drop the same column a second time before the materializing REORG, DB2 will return SQLCODE –205. You cannot unload from an image copy taken before the materializing REORG; utility message DSNU1227I will be issued. Finally, if you attempt to recover to a point-in-time (PIT) before the materializing REORG, the utility will fail with message DSNU556I.

Utility Enhancements

DB2 11 introduces a number of utility enhancements that improve availability and usability.

REORG Enhancements

A new SWITCHTIME option avoids the need for multiple jobs to control the start of the drain for the switch phase. You can specify a time at which the switch phase must occur, enabling you to automatically synchronize this phase with an application quiesce point or quiet time.

Prior to DB2 11, when you reorganized a subset of partitions, an image copy of the entire table space was taken. This can substantially increase the space required for image copy data sets. DB2 11 enables you to take partition-level image copies when reorganizing a subset of partitions. This includes tape support, but there is no support yet for STACK YES. It introduces an additional benefit for RECOVER processing by permitting parallel recoveries at the partition level. Keep in mind that exploiting this feature will require changes to your existing jobs.

DB2 11 enables even more control over REORG processing by adding RECLUSTER YES|NO support for REORG SORTDATA NO. The combination of SORTDATA NO and RECLUSTER NO bypasses sort and avoids using the clustering index to unload data. This can be useful for materializing REORG utilities, and it will speed up conversion to the extended-format RBA/LRSN. This feature is useful, but it saves time only if the data is already in clustering order. It is recommended that you do not use this feature on huge tables with a clustering index where the data rows are not already clustered, because the REORG could run for a long time. A new utility message indicates the method used to unload the table:

```
DSNU2904I DATA RECORDS WILL BE UNLOADED
VIA unload-method
```

Where *unload-method* is one of the following:

- CLUSTERING INDEX
- TABLE SCAN
- TABLE SPACE SCAN

DB2 11 introduces another REORG option, DRAIN_ALLPARTS YES (not the default), which has the potential to significantly reduce the impact on application availability. The objective of this option is to avoid deadlocks between drains and claims across non-partitioning indexes (NPIs) and data partitions when reorganizing a subset of the partitions.

This objective is achieved by momentarily obtaining the table space–level drain first, before draining the partitions and reorganizing indexes. This is more likely to be successful in getting a DRAIN to make the SWITCH than the old method of serially draining all the target partitions. DB2 11 customers have seen big reductions in the elapsed time needed to complete DRAIN and SWITCH processing, and REORGs should run with fewer problems using this feature.

To help customers get a better understanding of REORG progress, the new REORG utility message DSNU1138I provides information about drain begin and end times.

To enhance control of REORG, a new PARALLEL option helps you to control the degree of utility parallelism by specifying the maximum number of subtasks DB2 can start.

As always with migration, you should be aware of changed REORG defaults. For example, NOPAD YES is now the default for REORG DISCARD.

A new LOGRANGES NO option for REORG enables you to specify that REORG should bypass SYSLGRNX processing when determining what ranges of log records need to be processed during the LOG APPLY phase. This option should be used only when SYSLGRNX is known to be logically corrupt or must be reset.

The ability to run REORG REBALANCE SHRLEVEL(CHANGE) has already been touched on and is a big step in the right direction for 24/7 availability. REORG will also build a compression dictionary for empty partitions and will provide the ability to break-in on persistent threads running packages bound with RELEASE(DEALLOCATE).

DB2 11 delivers on a customer requirement that was raised as soon as universal table spaces were introduced, and that is partition pruning for UTS partition-by-growth (PBG) table spaces. Setting new ZPARM REORG_DROP_PBG_PARTS=ENABLE provides the option to physically remove empty UTS PBG partitions. This ZPARM is disabled by default, so you need to make a conscious decision to enable it because there is no support for PIT recovery to a point in time prior to the SWITCH phase for a table space where empty partitions have been pruned.

Automatic Mapping Tables

DB2 11 delivers an often-requested feature: automatic building of the mapping table that is used by REORG. The behavior differs depending on the DB2 mode, CM or NFM.

In DB2 11 CM, if there is an existing mapping table in the DB2 10 or DB2 11 format, it will be reused. If a mapping table does not exist, the mapping table will be created automatically and will be dropped at the end of REORG.

In DB2 11 NFM, if there is an existing mapping table in the DB2 11 format, it will be reused. If it's in the DB2 10 format, a new mapping table will be created automatically in the same database as the original mapping table. If a mapping table does not exist, one will be created automatically either in the database specified by ZPARM REORG_MAPPING_DATABASE or in the database specified by the MAPPING DATABASE option in the REORG job, or in DSNDB04.

This feature can be useful, but it must be used judiciously. You should still predefine and preserve mapping tables for regularly scheduled REORG jobs, in order to avoid SQL DDL contention on the catalog. It is also recommended that you use a single database, as specified in ZPARM REORG_MAPPING_DATABASE, for all mapping tables. You should modify the structure of your existing mapping tables to the DB2 11 format as part of the process of migrating to NFM, using the following SQL as a template:

```
ALTER TABLE TBMAP ALTER COLUMN LRSN SET DATA TYPE
CHAR(10) NOT NULL;
```

At the time of this writing, automatic mapping table APAR PI08339 is still open, and it is recommended that you wait for the APAR to be closed and apply the PTF, when available, if you want automated building of mapping tables.

RUNSTATS and RTS Enhancements

DB2 11 enables extra statistics to be collected inline by the REORG and LOAD utilities. This is acceptable, but inline statistics are estimates and do not provide the same quality of information as a standalone RUNSTATS utility.

When collecting inline statistics, customers sometimes get the message DSNU602I–"Statistics are not collected for nonpartitioned index" when running REORG PART. This situation can now be avoided by using the SORTNPSI option with the REORG job or by setting the REORG_PART_SORT_NPSI ZPARM to AUTO or YES. Either of these values can cause REORG to sort all the non-partitioned index keys before building the index, if the amount of data being reorganized relative to the size of the objects exceeds internal thresholds. YES specifies that if REORG estimates, based on the thresholds, that sorting all keys of the non-partitioned secondary indexes would improve the elapsed time, all keys are sorted. AUTO is very similar and causes all keys to be sorted if REORG estimates that elapsed time and CPU performance would be improved. The recommended option is to use AUTO, to maximize the probability of collecting inline statistics for NPIs.

One of the problems customers and IBM support have to deal with when resolving access path problems is that using different profiles or specifying different options over time can result in conflicting catalog statistics. This not only makes diagnosing access path problems difficult, but it can also mean that inaccurate information is used by the Optimizer when selecting an access path.

DB2 11 provides a new RESET ACCESSPATH option for RUNSTATS, which will reset all access path statistics for an object in the catalog. This does not affect space statistics in the catalog or Real-Time Statistics (RTS). Once the statistics have been reset, you then need to gather fresh access path statistics with RUNSTATS.

If you are using statistics profiles, make sure the statistics profile exists. If you get message DSNU1363I–"The stats profile for table *table-name* not found," indicating that the profile is not found, RUNSTATS will use fixed defaults that might be inappropriate. Another consideration when using statistics profiles is that there is no support for USE PROFILE with inline statistics in REORG and LOAD. In this case, you need to make sure the RUNSTATS options specified in the profile are consistent with those specified for REORG and LOAD inline statistics; otherwise, you risk ending up with conflicting statistics.

With DB2 and vendor products making more use of realtime statistics, there are customer demands for user control over the externalization of the RTS in-memory blocks. DB2 11 lets you do this with this new command:

```
-ACCESS DATABASE (DB) SP(TS) MODE(STATS)
```

RECOVER Enhancements

DB2 11 adds fast log apply (FLA) support for RECOVER INDEX. Previously, DB2 would wait until a log record was to be applied before reading the associated index page into the local buffer pool, where it would then be cached. Now, DB2 uses list prefetch for all the index pages that log apply will update before applying any log records. FLA for RECOVER INDEX has the potential for significant savings in elapsed time, and it means customers should now reconsider their recovery strategy for indexes, especially large NPIs. The decision to make is whether to run RECOVER INDEX in parallel with RECOVER TABLESPACE [PART] or to wait for RECOVER TABLESPACE [PART] to be completed and then run REBUILD INDEX. This enhancement has been taken back to DB2 9 and DB2 10 via APAR PI07694.

DB2 11's RECOVER TABLESPACE utility, when running under DIAGNOSE TYPE(607), provides an optimization when performing PIT recovery for a list of objects. Recovery of the objects is not necessary when there have been no updates after the PIT. This optimization is available only when performing PIT recovery with TOLOGPOINT or TORBA specified. It does not apply to log-only recoveries, RECOVER BACKPOUT, or recovers to current.

Performance and Scalability

DB2 11 delivers many performance and scalability improvements, and these have been discussed in detail in other Redbooks and white papers. We describe some of these briefly in this document, identifying what actions are required, if any, to benefit from them.

Performance Enhancements: No REBIND Needed (CM)

Many performance improvements are available in conversion mode (CM), even without rebinding your static SQL packages. The improvements described here are presented in no particular order, and the benefits you receive will be workload-dependent.

- More and more applications connect to DB2 via DRDA, so the Distributed Data Facility (DDF) performance improvements will be particularly welcome. DDF overhead can be significantly lower because DB2 11 reduces supervisor request block (SRB) scheduling for TCP/IP receive by exploiting new z/OS Communications Server capabilities. This feature can reduce CPU usage in the DIST address space and can reduce network latency. DRDA OLTP auto-commit performance is improved by enabling a DB2 for z/OS server to initiate commit after the result set is exhausted in the initial reply to the client. This enhancement can help reduce network flows, latency, and CPU consumption.

- DB2 11 exploits the z/OS V1.13 support for 64-bit code execution by moving xPROCs generated for fast column processing above the bar, reducing data movement costs.

- All SRB-mode DB2 system agents that are not response-time critical are zIIP-enabled, potentially reducing the total cost of ownership (TCO).

- CPU cycles are saved by using shared memory and avoiding the cross-memory overhead for creating log records in the log output buffer (OUTBUFF).

- Data decompression performance is improved by decompressing only the portion of the row needed either for predicate evaluation or for returning the columns back to the application.

- INSERT performance is critical for many customers, and DB2 11 continues to deliver improved performance in this area. Design changes mean that latch contention is reduced, and CPU is reduced for INSERT column processing and log record creation. More progress is made in data sharing by avoiding LRSN spin when creating log records. There is potential for improved INSERT performance because page fix/free is avoided when writing to the group buffer pool.

- Sort performance is improved, as is XML performance and performance for data-partitioned secondary index (DPSI) merge. There are also performance improvements when accessing objects with a large number of partitions.

- RELEASE(DEALLOCATE) execution is optimized so that it performs consistently better than RELEASE(COMMIT).

- Data replication capture performance is improved by the introduction of IFI 306 filtering capabilities to ensure that only the log records for the objects being replicated are presented to the capture task.

- Some workloads can experience performance degradation because of the growth in pseudo-deleted index entries. DB2 11 addresses this concern with the new automatic index pseudo delete-cleanup feature, which we describe in more detail later.

- Again for distributed applications, with ODBC/JDBC Type 2 performance improvements, Java stored procedure performance is improved by adding support for more efficient multithreaded JVMs and the 64-bit JVM.

- Performance of the ACCESS DATABASE command is improved by opening multiple objects in parallel.

- Declared global temporary table (DGTT) performance is improved by avoiding incremental binds, reducing the CPU overhead.

- With more and more applications exploiting Unicode, optimized P-procs for LIKE predicates against Unicode tables deliver improved performance.

- Other improvements include improved performance for ROLLBACK TO SAVEPOINT, zEC12 exploitation, other high n-way scalability improvements, and a number of data sharing performance improvements.

Performance Enhancements Requiring REBIND

Some performance benefits are available as soon as CM when you REBIND your static SQL packages, with or without APREUSE. These include:

- Most in-memory techniques

- Non-correlated subquery with mismatched length

- Select list do-once

- Column processing improvements

- Handling of row ID (RID) overflow to work file for data manager "set" functions

- Performance improvements for common operators

- DECFLOAT data type performance improvements

Some performance benefits are available as soon as CM when you REBIND your static SQL packages without APREUSE. In brief, these include:

- Query transformation improvements—less expertise required to write performant SQL

- Enhanced duplicate removal

- Some DPSI and page range performance improvements

- Optimizer CPU and I/O cost balancing improvements

Performance Enhancements Requiring DBA or Application Effort (NFM)

DB2 11 delivers a number of performance improvements that require DBA or application programmer effort:

- "Suppress-null" indexes

- The new PCTFREE FOR UPDATE attribute to reduce indirect references

- Global variables

- Optimizer externalization of missing/conflicting statistics

- Extended optimization—selectivity overrides (filter factor hints)

- The open data set limit raised to 200K

Optional Enhancements Requiring NFM and DBA Effort

There are two very important improvements, which we examine in more detail later, that require you to have migrated to NFM and also require DBA effort.

The first of these is optional, and that is to convert the bootstrap data set (BSDS) to exploit extended 10-byte RBAs using sample job DSNTIJCB. To do this, a -STOP DB2 MODE(QUIESCE) command is required.

The second enhancement, also optional, is to convert the DB2 catalog and directory table and index spaces to extended 10-byte RBA format using sample job DSNTIJCV. This conversion reorganizes all catalog and directory table spaces using SHRLEVEL CHANGE and can be split up to run the REORG utility jobs in parallel.

DB2 Lab Performance Measurement Summary

To get an idea of the performance improvements that are possible, Figure 2.3 summarizes measurements taken by the DB2 for z/OS development lab.

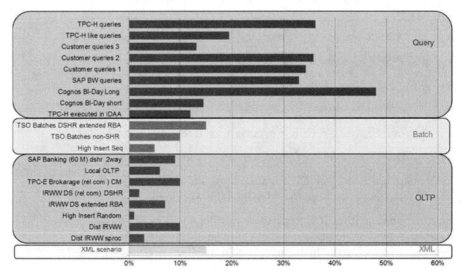

Figure 2.3: DB2 11 percent improvement over DB2 10

Example of Customer Performance Testing

Customers on the DB2 11 ESP dedicated a lot of time and resources to performance testing. This section reviews not only the results of one of these customers in some detail but also what measurements they took, and when they took them, so that you can exploit this methodology for your own evaluation of the performance benefits of DB2 11.

Starting with the times at which performance measurements were taken:

- DB2 10 NFM baseline
- DB2 11 CM before REBIND
- DB2 11 CM after REBIND
- DB2 11 NFM (no need for further REBIND)
- DB2 11 NFM after REORG (to migrate object to extended LRSN)
- DB2 11 NFM extended LRSN

When collecting performance measurements, you should follow the example of this customer and make sure the CPU numbers are normalized across those intervals (use CPU milliseconds per commit). It is relatively easy to combine statistics and accounting by stacking the various components of CPU resource consumption:

- *MSTR TCB / (commits + rollbacks)*

- *MSTR SRB / (commits + rollbacks)*

- *IRLM TCB / (commits + rollbacks)*

- *IRLM SRB / (commits + rollbacks)*

- *Average Class 2 CP CPU * occurrences / (commits + rollbacks)*

- *Average Class 2 SE CPU * occurrences / (commits + rollbacks)*

This customer tested both CICS transactions and batch jobs, and to understand the results you need to understand the workload.

Starting with the test CICS transaction profile, a variety of fetch-intensive transactions (e-bank logon, balance check, financial statement history, and account search) were used. On average, in SQL DML terms, these transactions performed:

- 3 x INSERT

- 7 x SELECT

- 5 x OPEN

- 103 x FETCH

Typical buffer pool activity saw 65 getpages and 13 synchronous reads. CPU consumption at DB2 10 NFM was 3.2 Class 1 msec and 2.3 Class 2 msec.

Figure 2.4 illustrates how 5 percent of the DB2 address space CPU was moved to zIIP engines simply by migrating to DB2 11 CM. A REBIND in CM reduced class 2 CPU time (CL2 CPU), and although this increased again in NFM, reorganizing the application objects and exploiting the extended LRSN combined to reduce DB2 address space and class 2 CPU times compared with DB2 10.

Figure 2.5 shows the effect on the DB2 system address spaces for the same workload. IRLM TCB time was so small it can't be seen in this graph, so it has been removed from the legend. The points to note here are a huge reduction in DBM1 TCB and SRB time, reduced MSTR SRB time, increased IRLM SRB time, and significant increases in the offload of DBM1 and MSTR CPU time to the zIIP engines.

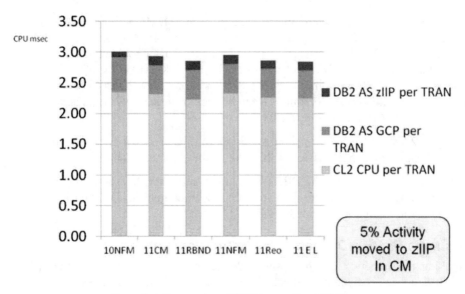

Figure 2.4: Progression of CICS transaction CPU time

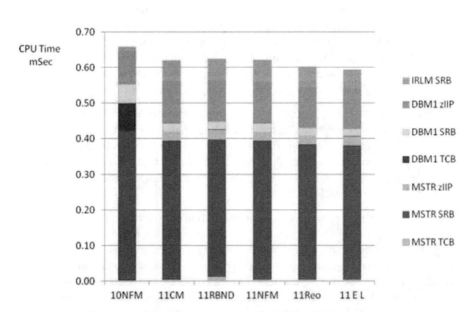

Figure 2.5: DB2 system address space CPU per CICS transaction

Moving on to the test batch job profile, typical SQL DML activity consisted of 4,528 commits, 37,613 deletes affecting 482,836 rows, 45,099 updates, 119,773 selects, 525,884 inserts, and 548,947 fetches. Buffer pool activity saw 4.8M getpage requests, 133K synchronous reads, and 57K dynamic prefetch requests. Class 1 CPU consumption was 69 seconds, and class 2 was 67 seconds. Class 1 elapsed time was 07:02 min. As can be seen from the DML figures, this application is INSERT and DELETE intensive.

Figure 2.6 shows the CPU time progression for the batch 0.70 job; the CPU time reduction with the extended RBA/LRSN is due to the elimination of LRSN spin.

Figure 2.7, the chart for the DB2 system address space CPU, shows two important things, the movement of processing to zIIP engines in CM and LRSN spin elimination with the extended LRSN/RBA.

Automatic Pseudo-Deleted Index Entry Cleanup

In looking at automatic cleanup of pseudo-deleted index entries in more detail, it is useful to recap on the impact of pseudo-deleted index entries to understand the importance of this feature.

As the number of pseudo-deleted index entries grows, the size of the index increases. This means more getpages and lock requests are required, and it leads to increased CPU costs and possibly longer elapsed times for SQL requests using index access. In addition, applications might encounter deadlocks and timeouts during INSERT/UPDATE/DELETE processing because of collisions with committed pseudo-deleted index entries and because of RID reuse by INSERT following DELETE.

Releases prior to DB2 11 include mechanisms to remove pseudo-deleted entries during mainline operations. Insert and delete operations try to remove these entries from index pages. SQL running with isolation level RR (repeatable read) can also remove pseudo-deleted entries. If any pages contain only pseudo-deleted index entries, DB2 tries to clean up these "pseudo-empty index pages" as part of DELETE processing.

Because most customers run with isolation CS (cursor stability), pseudo-deleted index entry cleanup was often not very effective using these methods, meaning customers had to use REORG INDEX. Doing so removes pseudo-empty index pages and pseudo-deleted entries that were not cleaned up by mainline processing. For some customers, this solution was problematic because of the extra CPU overhead of running REORG INDEX solely to clean up pseudo-deleted index entries and because of the difficulty in scheduling the REORG jobs.

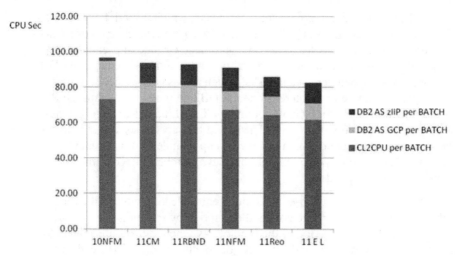

Figure 2.6: CPU time progression per batch

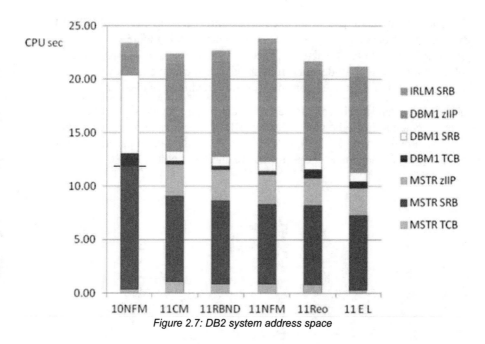

Figure 2.7: DB2 system address space

DB2 11 provides an autonomic solution in CM, which is by default automatically turned on for all indexes 24/7. This provides automatic cleanup of pseudo-deleted index entries in index leaf pages and automatic cleanup of pseudo-empty index pages. It is designed to cause minimal or no disruption for concurrent DB2 work. Cleanup is done under system tasks, which run as enclave SRBs and are zIIP-eligible. A parent thread (there is one per DB2 member) loops through RTS to find candidate indexes for cleanup, building a list of index leaf pages as they are accessed by index lookup or scan. The parent task schedules child threads to do the cleanup, but the child threads only clean up an index if it is already opened for INSERT, UPDATE, or DELETE on that DB2 member, to avoid making those indexes GBP-dependent.

Although automatic pseudo-deleted index entry cleanup runs all the time by default, customers can minimize potential disruption by managing the number of cleanup threads or by specifying the time of day when indexes are subject to cleanup. Customers can control the number of concurrent cleanup threads or even disable the function by using the new ZPARM INDEX_CLEANUP_THREADS. The function is disabled by setting the ZPARM to 0; the other allowable values range from 1 to 128, with 10 being the default.

To control automatic pseudo-deleted index entry cleanup at the individual index level, customers can insert entries into the new catalog table, SYSIBM.SYSINDEXCLEANUP. This lets you specify whether cleanup is enabled or disabled for an individual index, and if enabled, when cleanup is allowed to run. This provides very fine-grained control over the scheduling of cleanup.

Automatic pseudo-deleted index entry cleanup can provide significant benefits. Measurements showed up to 39 percent DB2 CPU reduction per transaction in DB2 11 compared with DB2 10, up to 93 percent reduction in pseudo-deleted entries in DB2 11, and consistent performance and less need of REORG.

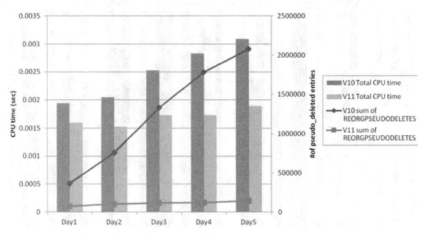

Figure 2.8: WAS portal workload—5 days performance

Figure 2.8: WAS portal workload—5 days performance

Performance Enhancements

A number of other performance enhancements have already been briefly discussed, and for some of these there are important usage considerations.

Q Replication Log Filtering

IFI 306 log filtering is targeted at Q Replication, but any replication product reading the DB2 log will benefit from this enhancement. This reduces the cost of IFI log read by allowed qualification of the objects being replicated by database ID/pageset ID (DBID/PSID). There are additional benefits if the objects are compressed. This enhancement moves filtering from the Q Replication capture task to the DB2 engine, with potential significant reduction in the number of log records replicated. To be able to exploit this feature, IBM InfoSphere Data Replication Q Replication or Change Data Capture 10.2.1 is required. Other replication products will also need modification to be able to benefit.

Archive Transparency

Archive transparency is a useful new feature that lets data that has been archived from the base table to a history table—either automatically by DB2 or by a user application—to be accessed via UNION ALL. This ability depends on the setting of the SYSIBMADM.GET_ARCHIVE global variable, without the need to modify the application program.

If you plan to use this feature, you need to carefully examine the additional cost of ORDER BY sort when accessing the archive. When the application fetches only a limited number of rows from the result set, the cost can increase significantly if the archive is also accessed. Customers will typically use this feature selectively on a case-by-case basis.

Optimizer Enhancements

The Optimizer delivers a number of important enhancements in DB2 11, providing improved performance for legacy application programs. There is a better chance of achieving matching index scan, and there is no need to rewrite SQL to get most of the improvements. However, it is still important to choose the right data type in your application program to avoid implicit casting, and it is still important to run RUNSTATS.

GROUP BY Grouping Sets

GROUP BY grouping sets is an important feature for data analysis, using the CUBE and ROLLUP functions delivered in DB2 11. All processing is performed in a single pass over the table, but there are some performance differences compared with the old GROUP BY with the same result set. Consider the following:

```
SELECT C1, COUNT(*) FROM T1 GROUP BY C1
```

In this case, sort is not performed if the access path uses an index with leading column C1. However, in the following case, a sort is always performed:

```
SELECT C1, COUNT(*) FROM T1 GROUP BY GROUPING SETS ((C1))
```

Extended LRBA/LRSN

This is one of the most significant changes in DB2 11, and if you are considering using it, there a number of implications for DB2 11 CM and DB2 10 NFM. To understand those, you first need to know about the extended LRBA/LRSN. (LRBA, or log relative byte address, is often used today instead of the more traditional RBA acronym.)

Before DB2 11, the LRBA/LRSN used a 6-byte format: x'LLLLLLLLLLLL'. The new 10-byte extended-format LRBA/LRSN has addressing capacity of 1 yottabyte, or $2**80$—an incredibly large number. The 10-byte extended-format LRSN with DB2 11 is in the form x'00LLLLLLLLLLLL000000', being extended on the right by 3 bytes to provide much finer timestamp granularity, and on the left by 1 byte to provide over 30,000 years of capacity. The 10-byte extended-format LRBA with DB2 11 is in the form x'00000000RRRRRRRRRRRR', being extended on the left by 4 bytes.

The LRBA/LRSN is recorded and found in a number of places:

- In the DB2 catalog: SYSCOPY, SYSxxxPART, . . .

- In the DB2 directory: SYSUTILX, SYSLGRNX, . . .

- In the BSDS: pointer, active and archive log values, . . .

- In the DB2 logs: active and archive logs

- In DB2 pagesets: the catalog and directory, and all user pagesets

Given the large number of places that the LRBA/LRSN is stored and accessed, there are some important considerations.

DB2 11 CM

DB2 internal coding deals with 10-byte extended-format LRBA/LRSN values only. The LRSN in utility output is shown in 10-byte extended format with precision '000000'—that is, extended on the right by 3 bytes of zeroes—except for the QUIESCE utility, which externalizes the LRSN in 10-byte extended format with precision 'nnnnnn'. The RECOVER utility handles 10-byte extended-format LRBA/LRSN input.

Column RBA_FORMAT in SYSIBM.SYSxxxPART is set to B for newly defined objects, or objects that have been reorganized or loaded with the REPLACE option. Possible values for RBA_FORMAT are B, blank, U, and E.

DB2 11 CM/DB2 10 NFM Coexistence in Data Sharing

There is full toleration for the 10-byte extended-format LRBA/LRSN value as input to the RECOVER utility. Sanity checks are included for "wrongly used 6-byte format LRBA/LRSN."

DB2 11 NFM

During migration to DB2 11 new-function mode via DSNTIJEN, catalog and directory table LRBA/LRSN columns are altered to the 10-byte extended format. SYSIBM.SYSLGRNX entries are now stored as 10-byte extended-format LRBA/LRSN values.

SYSIBM.SYSCOPY is updated to convert all LRBA/LRSN values for existing data to the 10-byte extended format with leading byte '00', precision '000000' for LRSN values, and right-justified with leading '00000000' for LRBA values. New data is stored in 10-byte extended format with precision 'nnnnnn'.

LRBA/LRSN values for all utilities are now in the 10-byte extended format, but LRBA/LRSN values are still written to the DB2 logs and to DB2 pagesets in the 6-byte format.

The BSDS can be converted to the 10-byte extended-format LRBA/LRSN only in NFM, via job DSNJCNVT. Be aware that once the BSDS has been converted to the new format, there is no way to convert back to the 6-byte format LRBA/LRSN. Once this happens, LRBA/LRSN values are written to DB2 logs of the subject DB2 member in the 10-byte extended format with precision 'nnnnnn'.

However, LRBA/LRSN values are still written to DB2 pagesets in the 6-byte format. To use the extended format, pageset conversion has to be done, although you can convert in either direction (10- to 6-byte or 6- to 10-byte). This means that, until a pageset is converted, LRSN spin can still happen. DSN1LOGP and REPORT RECOVER output will show the 10-byte extended format LRBA/LRSN, even though the 10-byte format is not externalized to the pagesets. DSN1PRNT will still report the 6-byte format for unconverted pagesets. Conversion of the pagesets can be done after entry to V11 NFM, in piecemeal fashion over an extended period of time.

The catalog and directory pagesets can be converted to "extended format," once in NFM, via REORG. This can be done at any time, regardless of the BSDS and user pageset formats. Once this is done, LRBA/LRSN values are written to the converted pagesets in the 10-byte extended format: the LRSN has precision 'nnnnnn' if the update is done on a DB2 member with a 10-byte extended-format BSDS; it has precision '000000' if the update in done in a member with a 6-byte format BSDS. Column RBA_FORMAT in SYSIBM.SYSxxxPART is updated to E for the converted objects. Be aware that LRSN spin could still happen for a DB2 member with a 6-byte format BSDS. The catalog and directory can be converted back to the 6-byte format, if needed at part level.

Just as for the catalog and directory, you can reorganize user pagesets to the extended-format LRBA/LRSN once in NFM. This can be done whenever you want, regardless of the BSDS or catalog and directory pageset formats. From this point onward, LRBA/LRSN values are written to the converted pagesets in the 10-byte extended format: the LRSN has precision 'nnnnnn' if the update is done on a DB2 member with a 10-byte extended format BSDS; it has precision '000000' if the update is done in a member with a 6-byte format BSDS. Column RBA_FORMAT in SYSIBM.SYSxxxPART is updated to E for the converted object. Again, be aware that LRSN spin could still happen for a DB2 member with a 6-byte format BSDS. As with the catalog and directory, user pagesets can be converted back to the 6-byte format.

User pageset conversion is done using REORG TABLESPACE or REORG INDEX, LOAD REPLACE or REBUILD INDEX with the RBALRSN_CONVERSION EXTENDED option, or if ZPARM OBJECT_CONVERTED is set to EXTENDED. Be aware that RECOVER TOCOPY using a 6-byte image copy can reset the format back to "basic."

ESP-Inspired Enhancements

ESP customer experience and feedback resulted in the delivery of several enhancements to improve usability:

- DSNJCNVT is prevented from converting the DB2 10 NFM BSDS to extended format.

- DB2 10 NFM supports 10-byte extended-format input.

- DB2 performs sanity checks to guard against invalid LRSN values—6-byte LRSN values with a leading byte of zeros—to prevent PIT recoveries using a bad LRBA/LRSN from failing. Instead, RC=8 is returned in the UTILINIT phase.

- Sanity checks are also performed in DB2 10 NFM when coexisting with DB2 11 CM.

- Support is provided for a NOBASIC value for the OBJECT_CONVERSION ZPARM to prevent pagesets already in extended format from being converted back to basic format. This also implies that EXTENDED and the catalog column for the object is <> 'E' (that is, conversion to the extended format is the default behavior).

- LRSN values are added to the archive log information in REPORT RECOVERY utility output.

- A technical white paper is being produced to explain about "6/10-byte LRBA/LRSN handling."

- Several enhancements have been made to the DB2 11 product documentation.

Recommended Best Practice Migration Strategy

Because there is a lot of flexibility in the way conversion to the 10-byte extended LRBA/LRSN can be done, many customers have asked for guidance as to the recommended best practice migration strategy, all the way from DB2 10 NFM to DB2 11 NFM, including conversion to the 10-byte extended LRBA/LRSN. The recommendation can be summarized at a high level as follows:

1. Run the pre-migration jobs and other steps to clean up DB2 10 NFM.
2. Migrate to DB2 11 CM.
3. Migrate to DB2 11 NFM.
4. Convert *all* BSDS of your data sharing group within *n* weekends.
5. Reorganize *all* directory and catalog pagesets to convert to the extended LRBA/LRSN format.
6. Set the OBJECT_CREATE and UTILITY_CONVERSION ZPARMs to EXTENDED:

   o New objects will be created in 10-byte extended format.

   o REORG, LOAD REPLACE, and REBUILD will convert user objects to extended format without the need to change utility control statements.

7. Reorganize all objects to convert them to the extended LRBA/LRSN format by executing your normal REORG jobs or some additional jobs:

   o Perform a regular check for progress in this task by selecting rows where RBA_FORMAT = E in SYSIBM.SYSxxxPART.

8. Once all objects have been converted, set the OBJECT _CONVERSION ZPARM to NOBASIC.

Converting a 10-Byte LRSN to a Timestamp

Customers are accustomed to converting 6-byte LRSN values to timestamps, but they are not familiar with doing so with a 10-byte LRSN. This section reviews the methods used by customers and then describes how to convert an extended LRSN in DB2 11 CM and DB2 11 NFM.

With DB2 10 NFM or less, use the TIMESTAMP function. The LRSN format is a 6-byte format, wherever used; for example, 'CBE2B5955DCF'. This format can be converted by:

```
SELECT TIMESTAMP(X'CBE2B5955DCF ' || X'0000') FROM ...
```

The practice in DB2 11 CM is very much the same. There are two possible LRSN formats: a 6-byte format in the logs, in the catalog and directory, and in data pages (e.g., 'CBE2B5955DCF') and a 10-byte format in all message and utility output, except for DSN1PRNT (e.g., '00CBE2B5955DCF086C00'). In both cases, the formats should be converted by:

```
SELECT TIMESTAMP(X'CBE2B5955DCF ' || X'0000') FROM ...
```

Note that the TIMESTAMP function requires an 8-byte string, hence the truncation of the 10-byte value.

Once in DB2 11 NFM, you should still use the TIMESTAMP function, but there are some subtle differences, and two use cases.

In the first use case, there are two possible LRSN formats: a 6-byte format for non-converted data pages, as reported by DSN1PRNT (e.g., 'CBE2B5955DCF') and a 10-byte format in the catalog and directory and in all message and utility output (e.g., '00CBE2B5955DCF086C00'. These formats can be converted by:

```
SELECT TIMESTAMP(X'CBE2B5955DCF ' || X'0000') FROM ...
```

A 6-byte LRSN can be used by "cut and paste," and a 10-byte LRSN can be used, if the first two digits are cut and digits 3 to 14 are used. However, the first two digits must be '00'; otherwise this conversion is *not* usable.

You can also use:

```
SELECT TIMESTAMP(BX'CBE2B5955DCF0000') FROM ...
```

or

```
SELECT TIMESTAMP(BX'CBE2B5955DCF086C') FROM ...
```

A 6-byte LRSN can be used by "cut and paste" and padded with '0000' on the right (the first example). A 10-byte LRSN can be used if first two digits are cut and digits 3 to 18 are used (the second example), but only if the first two digits are '00' ;otherwise, this conversion is *not* usable.

You have another option in DB2 11 NFM, using the "binary hex" function and APPLCOMPAT(V11R1) behavior:

```
SELECT TIMESTAMP(BX'00CBE2B5955DCF086C00000000000000')
FROM ...
```

A 6-byte LRSN can be used by "cut and paste," padded with '00' on the left and with '000000000000000000' on the right. A 10-byte LRSN can be used by "cut and paste" and right padded with '000000000000'. If desired, BX' can be replaced by BINARY(X' or VARBINARY(X'. This process converts a 10-byte LRSN to a timestamp. It works well, but your package needs to be bound with APPLCOMPAT(V11R1).

Other Performance Recommendations

There are several other important performance recommendations that you should take into account when migrating to DB2 11.

Make sure that HVCOMMON—64-bit common—configured in IEASYSxx is large enough to accommodate the log output buffer, which now uses 1 MB page frames. In practice, this means you should configure additional storage in the 1 MB LFAREA (IEASYSxx) for maximum benefit.

Remember that LRSN spin avoidance requires that both the BSDS and the user objects are converted to the expanded LRBA/LRSN in NFM. If this is an issue for you, you should prioritize converting the objects that are affected by LRSN spin for conversion. Once the conversion process is under way, you should monitor log I/O performance, as the log record size increases. The increase depends on a number of factors, including row length, the number of columns updated, column length, and so on. Customers have observed an increase in log record size from 3 percent to 40 percent following BSDS conversion.

It is essential to make sure there is enough zIIP capacity available before migrating to DB2 11 CM. The zIIP "Help Function" IIPHONORPRIORITY should be set to YES in case there is a shortage of zIIP capacity. You should continue to monitor zIIP capacity thereafter, focusing on zIIP redirect back to the general-purpose processors because this is a more important measure than zIIP utilization.

In DB2 9, reclassification of sequential buffers read in by prefetch to random if they were accessed by a random GETPAGE was discontinued. This change is reversed in DB2 11, so pages that have been prefetched are again reclassified as random after a random GETPAGE. This means you might need to re-evaluate the VPSEQT setting for some local buffer pools where it has been increased because of the change introduced in DB2 9.

There are two other changes in the area of buffer management. Previously, pages read in by the COPY utility were managed according to the most recently used (MRU) algorithm to avoid flooding the buffer pool with pages read by COPY and damaging the hit ratio. This approach is now used more extensively; for example, pages read by the UNLOAD utility, the unload phase of REORG, and the unload phase of REBUILD are all now managed using the MRU algorithm.

Second, using large frames to back buffer pools was tied to page-fixing the buffers to save CPU by avoiding page-fix and page-free for dataset and coupling facility I/O. DB2 11 enables more granular control by introducing the new FRAMESIZE parameter, which is independent of the PGFIX parameter, and lets you specify a page frame of 4 KB, 1 MB, or 2 GB.

Performance Summary

When estimating what kind of performance improvement you can expect in DB2 11, you have to take into account a number of factors. DB2 11 certainly presents an opportunity for improved performance for legacy application programs, but your mileage will vary based on the SQL profile of your application workload because the benefits introduced by certain features are specific to certain workloads. While immense CPU savings were observed for some workloads, highly optimized static SQL and/or simple SQL may not see much benefit.

You should expect to see more benefit for a workload characterized by more complex SQL; that is, SQL that does more than read a single row by primary key. Therefore, it is important that you do not sell (or buy) the CPU savings before they have been measured and validated for your particular workload over a period of time.

Other Enhancements

The final section of this document discusses two other enhancements that will be of interest to some customers: removing package security vulnerabilities and archive transparency.

Remove Package Security Vulnerabilities

To understand what this enhancement offers, it's useful to describe the problem use case. Consider the case where each main application routine has its own plan, and where the name of the program and the plan are the same. All packages are bound into a single collection, and each plan is bound with PKLIST(col.*). If the EXECUTE privilege is granted on one plan, the authid/user with that privilege can effectively run any main application program.

DB2 11 solves this dilemma by introducing a new BIND PLAN option, PROGAUTH, which is supported by a new catalog table, SYSIBM.DSNPROGAUTH. To ensure that a main program M can only be executed with plan P, you need to insert a row into SYSIBM.DSNPROGAUTH with column PROGNAME set to 'M', PLANNAME set to 'P', and ENABLED set to 'Y'. To make this specification, you then need to bind plan P using the new option PROGAUTH(ENABLE).

Archive Transparency

Archive transparency provides the capability to create an archive (or history) table and connect the base table to the archive table. This is done using the ALTER TABLE DDL statement with the ENABLE ARCHIVE clause. This technique requires the archive table and base table to have exactly the same columns. No additional columns are allowed, such as archive timestamp.

If you set the new SYSIBMADM.MOVE_TO_ARCHIVE global variable to either 'Y' or 'E', DB2 automatically moves deleted rows to the archive table. If the value is 'Y', any attempted update to rows in the archive-enabled base table will fail with SQLCODE –20555. On the other hand, if it is set to 'E', the attempted update will work for active rows in the base table, but not for rows in the archive table. In either case, deletion of active rows in the base table will result in those rows being inserted into the archive table.

If the SYSIBMADM.MOVE_TO_ARCHIVE global variable is set to 'N', any rows deleted from the base table are lost. Because 'N' is the default, it's important to make sure the global variable is set to 'Y' or 'E' if you want DB2 to automatically move deleted base table rows to the archive table.

Another new global variable, SYSIBMADM.GET_ARCHIVE, must be set to 'Y' for a query to search both the rows from the base table and those from the archive table. Remember that any update applies only to active rows in the base table, so any subsequent query might see updated rows from the base table, and not updated rows from the archive table.

A new package BIND option is available, ARCHIVESENSITIVE (YES|NO), with NO being the default. Again, this only affects whether or not rows are read from the archive table as well as the base table. Deleted rows are moved to the archive table only if the MOVE_TO_ARCHIVE global variable is set correctly.

If you run REORG DISCARD on the base table, REORG generates a LOAD statement that can be used to load the discarded rows into the archive table. The DISCARD dataset can then be used as input to the LOAD utility, and in most cases this is the right course of action.

There are two important considerations. First, dynamic scrollable cursors cannot be used with archive-enabled tables. Second, the package owner must have the WRITE privilege for the respective global variables to be able to set them.

For More Information

To learn more about IBM DB2 11 for z/OS, please contact your IBM representative or IBM Business Partner, or visit *ibm.com/software/data/db2/zos/family*.

In addition, IBM Global Financing can help you acquire the IT solutions that your business needs in the most cost-effective and strategic way possible. We'll partner with credit-qualified clients to customize an IT financing solution to suit your business goals, enable effective cash management, and improve your total cost of ownership. IBM Global Financing is your smartest choice to fund critical IT investments and propel your business forward. For more information, visit *ibm.com/financing*.

DB2 11 Resources

A number of resources are available for you to use when migrating to DB2 11 or when exploiting the performance benefits.

- The IBM Information Center/Knowledge Center

- The *IBM DB2 11 Technical Overview* Redbook (SG24-8180)

- IBM DB2 11 for z/OS home page:
  ibm.com/software/data/db2/zos/family/db211

    o DB2 11 announcement letter, webcasts, and customer case studies

    o Whitepaper: *DB2 11 for z/OS: Unmatched Efficiency for Big Data and Analytics*

    o Whitepaper: *How DB2 11 for z/OS Can Help Reduce Total Cost of Ownership*

    o DB2 11 Migration Planning Workshop

DB2 10 Migration to DB2 11 and Application Compatibility

Plan your transition for business results

by Chris Crone and Jay Yothers

Migration to IBM® DB2® 11 for z/OS® can be much easier and faster when compared with migration to DB2 10. The product stability of DB2 11 has also been demonstrated to be even stronger than DB2 10. During the Early Support Program (ESP), stability was so solid that organizations started deploying in a customer production environment.

The restructuring of the catalog in DB2 11 is much less extensive and centers around the new ability to support extended log record sequence number (LRSN) values. Laboratory testing and responses from customers enrolled in the DB2 11 ESP suggest that catalog migration might be as much as 15 times faster in DB2 11 than in DB2 10. Of course, every DB2 environment is different. The duration of the migration process tends to center around recovery information that is maintained in the catalog and directory. If the amount of recovery information is reduced or maintained at a reasonable level, the duration of migration to DB2 11 can be minimized.

Second, and more important, DB2 has now separated the requirement to migrate your applications from the process of migrating your DB2 subsystem. Through the use of this important new capability—called *application compatibility*—you can migrate your DB2 10 subsystem to DB2 11 without making changes to your applications to deal with any SQL changes or incompatibilities presented by DB2 11. After you complete your migration to the new release, you can address the use of any of these incompatibilities surgically and precisely.

Migration Prerequisites

The hardware prerequisite for DB2 11 is an EC12, z196, or z10™ processor supporting z/Architecture®. Although DB2 11 will run well on a z10 or z196, it was designed to take advantage of the unique capabilities of the EC12 machine.

In terms of software prerequisites, DB2 11 requires:

- z/OS V1.13 Base Services (5694-A01) or later

- DFSMS V1R13

   o New data sets for the DB2 catalog and directory continue to be SMS-managed in DB2 11. If you choose to condition the catalog and directory for extended LRSNs by running the DSNTIJCV job described later in this paper, the result will be that the entire catalog and directory will come to reside in SMS-managed space.

- Language Environment Base Services

- z/OS Version 1 Release 13 Security Server (RACF®)

- IRLM Version 2 Release 3, which is shipped with DB2 11 for z/OS

- z/OS Unicode Services and appropriate conversion definitions

- IBM InfoSphere® Data Replication (IIDR) 10.2.1, if you want IIDR to make use of the extended LRSNs that may be written to the log by DB2 11

- DB2 Connect™ 10.5 Fix Pack 2

   o Although this fix pack is listed along with the other prerequisites, it is not a hard prerequisite. DB2 11 can run with any level of DB2 Connect that is currently in service. However, if you want to take full advantage of the performance improvements in DB2 11 when dealing with DB2 Connect, it should be at least at 10.5 Fix Pack 2.

The final software prerequisite for migrating to DB2 11 for z/OS is that your current DB2 subsystem must be running DB2 10 in new-function mode. Migration to DB2 11 from any other release of DB2 is not supported.

As with prior releases, DB2 11 provides a job called DSNTIJPM (PM for pre-migration), which produces a number of reports that will help you prepare for migrating to DB2 11. An identical copy of this job is shipped in DB2 10, although its name there is DSNTIJPB. Therefore, you should already have a copy of DSNTIJPB that you can begin to run now to help prepare for migrating to DB2 11 in the future.

Modes of Migration

The migration modes that we have become accustomed to in prior releases exist in DB2 11, as well. These are conversion mode (CM), enabling-new-function mode (ENFM), and new-function mode (NFM). These modes are somewhat simplified from DB2 10 because migration to DB2 11 can be from DB2 10 only, so there is no need to augment the mode names with the number of the release from which the DB2 subsystem was migrated.

Conversion mode is the first mode you enter when migrating to DB2 11. You can remain in CM for as long as you like; however, no new SQL function is available in CM. Fallback to DB2 10 and data sharing coexistence with DB2 10 are supported only while in CM. IBM's recommendation is to stay in CM for a month or two to possibly include some major event, such as quarter-end or year-end processing. The goal would be to convince yourself that DB2 11 will support your environment at least as well as DB2 10 did.

When you are satisfied that DB2 11 will support your environment, you can move on from CM into enabling-new-function mode. In ENFM, DB2 conditions the catalog and directory for the use of new function. To enter ENFM, no DB2 10 subsystems can be active in a data sharing group. After you enter ENFM, you can no longer fall back to or coexist with DB2 10. As with CM, no new SQL function is available in ENFM.

When the catalog and directory have been conditioned for new functionality by the ENFM process, you can enter new-function mode. In NFM, all new functionality is available. When you enter NFM, you can begin to deal with any incompatibilities that the application compatibility traces identify and make changes to your applications to use the new DB2 11 functions. Some changes can be introduced or preconditioned only once you are in NFM (for instance, you might want to use CHAR9 to deal with the V10 CHAR issue; you can't use CHAR9 until you are in NFM). However, you can identify and deal with many of the issues prior to this. Entering NFM in a data sharing environment rebuilds the shared communications area in the coupling facility to prepare for the use of extended LRSNs.

DB2 11 also provides the star (*) modes. When you have moved beyond CM in the sequence of migration, you can return to CM from either ENFM or NFM. However, when you do so, DB2 attaches the star to the mode (CM*) to indicate that you have actually been beyond CM at some point in the past and therefore you can no longer fall back to or coexist with DB2 10. Similarly, when you have moved beyond ENFM into NFM, you can return to ENFM. However, when you do so, DB2 attaches the star to the mode (ENFM*) to indicate that you have actually been in NFM at some point in the past.

Functional Availability

When we talk about out-of-the box performance enhancements, we're talking about those enhancements that are available in CM after a rebind without the use of the APREUSE option. However, we always get questions about what is available when, with or without a rebind. In an effort to answer some of those questions, let us list some of the performance enhancements that are available at various times. Please keep in mind that these lists are dynamic; items could possibly move from one list to another with the application of maintenance.

First, these are the DB2 11 performance enhancements that are available with no rebind at all:

- Distributed Data Facility (DDF) performance improvements

- xPROCs above the bar

- zIIP enablement for all SRB-mode DB2 system agents that are not response-time critical

- Avoidance of cross-memory overhead for writing log records

- Data decompression performance improvement

- INSERT performance improvement

- Automatic index pseudo-delete cleanup

- ODBC/JDBC type 2 performance improvements

- Java stored procedure multithreading improvements

- Sort performance improvements

- Data-partitioned secondary index (DPSI) performance improvements for merge

- Performance improvements with a large number of partitions

- XML performance improvements

- Optimized RELEASE(DEALLOCATE) execution so that it consistently performs better than RELEASE(COMMIT)

- IFI 306 filtering capabilities to improve replication capture performance

- Utilities performance improvements

- Enhanced ACCESS DATABASE command performance

- Declared global temporary table performance improvements

- P-procs for LIKE predicates against Unicode tables

- Improved performance for ROLLBACK TO SAVEPOINT

- zEC12 exploitation

- Latch contention reduction and other high n-way scalability improvements

- Data sharing performance improvements

Next is a list of the additional performance enhancements available with a rebind using APREUSE:

- Most in-memory techniques
- Non-correlated subquery with mismatched length
- Select list do-once
- Column processing improvements
- Row ID (RID) overflow to work file handled for aggregate functions in stage 1 predicates
- Performance improvements for common operators
- DECFLOAT data type performance improvements

The next list of additional performance enhancements are available with a rebind but without using APREUSE. This group, combined with the two lists above, comprise the enhancements that provide the featured CPU reduction:

- Query transformation improvements so that less expertise is required to write SQL code that performs well
- Enhanced duplicate removal
- DPSI and page range performance improvements
- Optimizer CPU versus I/O cost balancing improvements

The next group of items requires NFM and some actions by DBAs, application programmers, or both:

- Suppress-null indexes
- New PCTFREE FOR UPDATE attribute to reduce indirect references
- Global variables
- Optimizer externalization of missing or conflicting statistics
- Extended optimization—selectivity overrides (filter factor hints)

Optional Migration Processing

All of the information above tells the complete migration story. However, some customers may consider preparing their entire DB2 subsystem for the use of extended (10-byte) LRSNs throughout. This is completely optional at this point. To prepare for extended LRSNs requires modifications to the bootstrap data set (BSDS) of a non-data sharing DB2 subsystem or to the BSDS of every member of a data sharing group, as well as a change to all the data pages in the catalog and directory.

Job DSNTIJCB will convert an individual DB2 subsystem's BSDS to support extended LRSNs. The DB2 subsystem must be stopped so that its BSDS can be converted. Stopping the subsystem with the MODE(QUIESCE) option is recommended. After DSNTIJCB is run, the DB2 subsystem can be restarted. You then need to run DSNTIJCB for the BSDSs of all the members of a data sharing group. This can be done one member at a time to provide continuous availability of the data sharing group.

Job DSNTIJCV changes the catalog and directory pages by performing a reorganization of each and every table space in the catalog and directory, one at a time, with the SHRLEVEL CHANGE option. These reorganizations run SHRLEVEL CHANGE; therefore, normal activity need not be curtailed while this job runs. Because the job reorganizes the entire catalog and directory, it can take quite a while to be completed. You can reduce the duration of the job by eliminating unused objects, plans, and packages and by reducing the statistics and recovery history to a reasonable level. Even so, you should expect this job to run for a number of hours.

To reduce the elapsed time, you can break up the job into a number of jobs that you can run in parallel. The very first step conditions SYSTUILX, which must be empty at the time, meaning no utilities can be running.

The Essentials of Migration

Catalog migration to DB2 11 for z/OS is much easier and takes far less time compared with migrating to DB2 10. The performance enhancements that DB2 11 may provide are impressive, especially when one considers that this is on top of the CPU reductions that could be realized when migrating to DB2 10. Also, the improved DB2 11 stability was sufficient for us to see DB2 11 deployed in a customer production environment prior to GA.

The migration process follows the same well-traveled path of prior releases, except that the migration steps themselves take far less time than in DB2 10. Finally, with the ability to remove the task of dealing with potential incompatible changes to applications until after migration is complete, the migration process is further simplified.

Application Compatibility in DB2 11 for z/OS

DB2 11 for z/OS introduces the concept of application compatibility to simplify migration. Businesses must decide how to take advantage of this new capability to identify changes they might need to make to applications that may be affected by incompatible changes in DB2 11.

Description of the Problem

There are many reasons for change. There are IBM standards and industry standards for SQL that DB2 for z/OS must be compliant with. Resolving compliance issues sometimes introduces an incompatible change that may have a negative effect on existing applications.

An example of an incompatibility introduced in DB2 10 is a change to the CHAR function. To conform to the SQL standard, DB2 10 changed the way in which CHAR and VARCHAR built-in functions format decimal data. The same was true for CAST specifications with decimal input and a CHAR or VARCHAR result type. In addition to complying with the SQL standard, this change made DB2 for z/OS more consistent with other members of the IBM DB2 family. The change was documented as an incompatible change, and the impact to customers was, in some cases, severe.

The impact of this change was mitigated in DB2 10 with APARs PM66095 and PM65722. In addition, DB2 11 for z/OS introduced CHAR9 and VARCHAR9 functions to provide the behavior of V9 CHAR and VARCHAR functions while still allowing new client and vendor applications to take advantage of standard SQL behavior for the CHAR and VARCHAR functions.

A different example of incompatible behavior was the introduction of implicit casting in DB2 10. This new function (available in NFM) enables implicit casting between numeric and string data types. This capability was added to DB2 to help applications that are primarily string-based (e.g., Perl, PHP, REXX).

The following SQL statement provides a simple example of this capability:

```
CREATE TABLE T1 C1 INTEGER;

    INSERT INTO T1 VALUES ('123');   ← Fails in DB2 9; works in DB2 10 NFM
```

In addition, function-resolution rules and the functions themselves were changed in DB2 10 to allow character and numeric data to be handled interchangeably. Again, this can be demonstrated with a simple example:

```
SELECT  123 || 'abc' FROM T1;   ← Fails in DB2 9; works in DB2 10 NFM
```

By definition, most new function is incompatible with existing behavior in some way. At the very least, it results in the removal of an SQLCODE that previously indicated the function was unavailable (either syntactically or semantically).

Impact to Customers

When they learn about changes in SQL or XML behavior, customers often have difficulty figuring out the impact of a single change to thousands of applications. DB2 has historically tried to limit incompatible changes. However, when these changes are necessary, we have tried to implement them at a release boundary to give customers time to do the necessary planning. IBM recognizes that trying to coordinate application changes as part of a release migration is difficult because making application changes is not practical and might even be impossible during the migration to a new release.

Solution Requirements

Discussions with customers have led to the following requirements that need to be addressed in any solution to help customers migrate to new releases of DB2 with as little application impact as possible:

- Do not force application changes to address incompatible SQL changes on a release boundary.

- Allow changes to be introduced at the application (package) level.

- Give customers more warning and time to address incompatible changes.

- Provide a mechanism to identify applications that need to be analyzed for potential impact by incompatible behavior.

Solution

DB2 will continue to limit SQL Data Manipulation Language (DML) and XML incompatibilities when possible. This is a basic tenet of simplifying migration and reducing customer impact. DB2 will also provide mechanisms to identify and make changes to affected applications (packages). To ensure that this capability provides reasonable time for customers to make these changes, this mechanism will promote support for up to two back-level releases (N–2). For example[1]:

- DB2 11 supports DB2 10 and DB2 11.

- DB2 _2 supports DB2 10 and DB2 11 and DB2 _2.

- DB2 _3 supports DB2 11 and DB2 _2 and DB2 _3.

- DB2 _4 supports DB2 _2 and DB2 _3 and DB2 _4.

Solution Details

DB2 11 introduces a new PACKAGE bind (BIND/REBIND) option (APPLCOMPAT) and a special register that applies to anything that has a package (including stored procedures, user-defined functions, and triggers. The new APPLCOMPAT bind option applies to static SQL, and it is the default for the special register (CURRENT APPLICATION COMPATIBILITY), which applies to dynamic SQL. The default behavior for this special register in a stored procedure or user-defined function is to not inherit this special register. For distributed applications, this special register can either be set in the properties file for (ODBC/JDBC/.NET) drivers, or controlled by the DSN_PROFILE tables for the application.

---

[1] DB2 _2, DB2 _3, and DB2 _4 are theoretical releases used in this example strictly for demonstrative purposes. This is not a commitment by IBM to actually produce any of these releases.

ALL SQL DML and XML changes are controlled by the new bind and special register options. This includes:

- New SQL function

- Incompatible SQL changes, such as:

  o Function-resolution rules

  o Result type changes

  o SQLCODE changes

  o Built-in function (BIF) changes

Interaction with NFM

In a migration or co-existence environment, the purpose of NFM is to prevent creation of an application or use of a DB2 function or capability that would prevent falling back to a previous release of DB2. Historically (since DB2 V8), when you move to NFM, you are able to use all new function and capability but can no longer fall back to the prior release.

By adding the new APPLCOMPAT option, DB2 provides a way to increase the consistency of application behavior across releases of DB2. As such, APPLCOMPAT for the current release (DB2 11) cannot be specified until a DB2 subsystem has reached NFM. When in NFM, you can specify either APPLCOMPAT(V11R1) or APPLCOMPAT(V10R1). In future releases, two down-level releases will be supported, in addition to the current release. Figure 3.1 illustrates this pattern.

Identifying Applications That Need to Be Examined

DB2 10 introduced IFCID 366 to help customers identify potential issues with applications. DB2 11 builds on this capability by adding IFCID 376 and package level accounting summary bit QPACINCOMAT to more easily find specific SQL statements that need to be examined.

QPACINCOMAT provides information that at least one SQL statement in a package needs to be examined before being bound in a newer release. Customers can use package level accounting to help them determine which applications (packages) need to be examined. Then they can use IFCID 376 to do a deeper dive.

IFCID 376 provides function similar to rollup accounting, where statements will only be listed once, regardless of the number of times they are executed for the life of the trace. Customers can run this trace once they have migrated to DB2 11. When an application is executed in APPLCOMPAT(V10R1), and potential incompatible issues will be flagged and information assist the customer in identifying the application and the SQL statement that need to be examined to determine if the application is affected by the change.

Normal Migration DB2 11 → DB2 _2

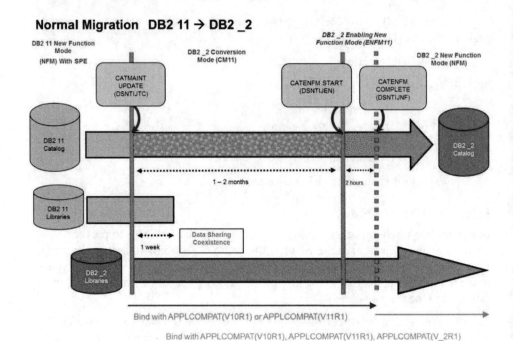

Figure 3.1: This diagram depicts the migration pattern for DB2.

New Reserved Words

Every release of DB2 adds new reserved words. For example, DB2 11 adds the reserved word ARRAY_EXISTS (a new reserved word for a predicate). DB2 has made great strides in enhancing the parser to make new reserved words be reserved only in context. This reduces, but does not eliminate, impact to customers as they migrate from release to release.

For example, in V10 and V11, the following statements work fine because:

- In DB2 10, ARRAY_EXISTS is not a reserved word.

- In DB2 11, ARRAY_EXISTS is treated as an identifier.

```
CREATE TABLE T1 (ARRAY_EXISTS INT);   ← No syntax error
INSERT INTO T1 VALUES (11);

CREATE FUNCTION UDF2 () RETURNS INT
  BEGIN
    DECLARE X INT;
    SELECT ARRAY_EXISTS INTO X FROM T1;   ← No syntax error
    RETURN X * 2;
  END!
SELECT UDF2() FROM SYSIBM.SYSDUMMY1!   ← Returns 22
```

In contrast, the following statements work in DB2 10, but the syntax shown in bold fails in DB2 11:

```
CREATE FUNCTION ARRAY_EXISTS (PARM1 CHAR(3), PARM2 INT)   ← No error in
RETURNS CHAR(1)                                              V10 or V11
  BEGIN
    RETURN SUBSTR(PARM1,PARM2,1);
  END!
COMMIT!

CREATE FUNCTION UDF1 () RETURNS INT
  BEGIN
    DECLARE X CHAR(3) DEFAULT 'ABC';
    IF ARRAY_EXISTS(X,1) = 'A' THEN   ← OK in V10; –104 in V11
      RETURN 1;
    ELSE
      RETURN 2;
    END IF;
  END!

SELECT UDF1() FROM SYSIBM.SYSDUMMY1;
```

New Reserved Word Solution

With DB2 11, IBM added code (in an APAR) to DB2 10 to:

- Identify where DB2 11 keywords would cause a failure

- Issue IFCID 366 to alert customers of this issue

Because new reserved words are reserved only in context, we expect that most customers will identify few or no issues, but this function allows customers to move forward with confidence. APAR PM84769/UK94459 was closed in 2Q2013. Three words are checked, in context: ARRAY_EXISTS, CUBE, and ROLLUP.

Pre-Migration Planning

In DB2 11, any issues we can detect with SQL in the pre-migration job, DSNTIJPM, will continue to be flagged. DB2 11 will also continue to flag any issues (with warnings or error codes) that are detected with SQL in DSNTIJPM. In the future, during migration to the release that comes after DB2 11, DSNTIJPM will flag:

- Warnings in DB2 11+1 for any packages that are bound with APPLCOMPAT(V10R1)

- Warnings in DB2 11+2 for any packages that are bound with APPLCOMPAT(V11R1)

- Serious errors in DB2 11+2 for any packages that are bound with APPLCOMPAT(V10R1) or lower; these packages will be inoperative when migration to that following release (DB2 11 + 2) occurs

What's Not Part of This Solution

This solution does not include changes to SQL function that resulted from customer-reported issues (PMRs and APARs). Customer-initiated APARs can result in differences in SQL behavior. Although these changes almost always correct a defect in the product, the changed behavior can affect the results other customers see.

Summary

With the APPLCOMPAT bind option, DB2 provides a foundation to separate release migration from application changes that may be necessary to enable an application to take advantage of function in a new release.

DB2 is providing two releases of backward-compatible behavior to enable customers to migrate more quickly to a new release, with confidence that applications will behave the same in the new release as they have in the previous one.

Customers can use the tracing capabilities provided in DB2 11 to identify applications that may need to change. If any changes are needed, customers have two releases to make the necessary changes to the affected applications.

Case Study:

BMW Group Develops Eco-Friendly Innovation for Smart Drivers with IBM

Managing a mountain of data driven by apps for drivers, sustainability, and eco-drive initiatives

Established in 1916 and headquartered in Munich, Germany, BMW Group is one of the world's largest and most successful car manufacturers. Operating in 150 countries, the company employs more than 107,000 people.

Steering Toward Smarter, Eco-Friendly Motoring

The pressing demand for sustainability and smarter solutions across every industry has prompted BMW Group to review its strategy in light of dynamic market trends and, ultimately, changes in people's lifestyles.

To address these challenges, BMW Group formulated a project named Strategy Number ONE, currently in the "Next Movement" phase. This focuses on sustainable solutions such as car sharing, on eco-friendly vehicles such as the BMW i3 featuring eDrive technology, and on smart mobility services such as the "Park at my house" smart phone app for faster and cheaper parking.

In the back office, the business innovation programs produced ever-greater data processing and information management workloads. For example, the smart phone app generates new data—and lots of it—that must be stored, analyzed, and exploited. Existing IT systems struggled to manage the increase in throughput, and data volumes started to rocket, requiring a great deal of maintenance and support time from IT staff that should otherwise be profitably deployed to future-facing development tasks.

Starting Up the Business Engines with IBM

BMW Group is a large user of IBM® DB2® technology, with over 130 IBM DB2 subsystems, belonging to more than 40 data sharing groups and spread over eight virtual servers on IBM System z® servers.

On the announcement of Version 11 of IBM DB2 for z/OS®, BMW Group immediately chose to join the Early Support Program (ESP). Previous experience of ESP with DB2 10 had shown that early adoption would bring early benefits, and BMW Group was keen to take advantage of the new DB2 features.

IBM DB2 11 for z/OS, the latest version of IBM DB2, features cost-effective and time-saving tools and also offers simpler, faster migration that ultimately translates into minimum risk of business disruption. DB2 11's enhanced analytics, forecasting, and reporting capabilities make it a central tool to boost the business innovation strategy that the company wants to achieve.

BMW Group's global operations and activities are served by its Munich data center, which means that systems must be available 24/7. Because peak workload times vary globally, the company needs to ensure that workload is optimized to meet local demand in all 150 countries.

A BMW Group manager explains, "We operate in a very dynamic 24/7 environment, and we often have to update our applications while they continue to operate. With DB2 11, the combination of the ability to break into persistent threads and the enhanced dynamic schema change capabilities allow us to react to business requirements more quickly and with less operational impact. We can plan, implement, and commit changes without business interruption—a major advantage for global operations."

Gaining Efficiency with DB2 11

Another big concern for the company was to find a way to decrease its CPU usage. The manager states, "With such a huge workload to handle, total capacity is an issue. Some workload peaks are unavoidable, which can lead to a negative impact on service delivery. The smart phone app and "green" car would add potentially huge extra volumes of work and presented us with complex challenges around data management, performance, and cost."

BMW Group realized that the enhanced data decompression capacity within DB2 11—much faster than the previous software version—would enable the company to optimize certain online transaction processing, query workloads, and data sharing and provide up to 15 percent CPU savings when running the queries against compressed tables. This would allow greater workload to be processed within the same processor footprint and at a greater speed, delivering cost efficiency and productivity gains right from the DB2 11 box.

"Despite still being very early in our performance testing, we have already seen CPU reductions of 8 to 13 percent on some of the workloads, thanks to the more efficient decompression algorithms that IBM DB2 allows us to run," adds the manager.

Gearing Up for a Successful Automotive Future

With IBM DB2 11 for z/OS in place, BMW Group is now fully ready to continue its innovation journey. Plans include deployment of an IBM zEnterprise EC12 server, to support cloud delivery models, forecast to increase server productivity even further.

"IBM DB2 11 has helped us to eliminate the performance and throughput challenges associated with our business innovation plans, and we can now easily cope with our ever-growing workload," concludes the manager.

"We are very excited to complete our new environment with the introduction of the IBM zEnterprise EC12 server and are looking forward to taking advantage of the extended possibilities that this presents. With the IBM infrastructure in place, we will be able to completely focus our attention and efforts on exploring clients' requests for innovation in the automotive sector."

Case Study:

JN Data Gets the Early Adopter Advantage for Its Growing Business

Using advanced automation and new functionality in DB2 11 for z/OS to provide outstanding service

JN Data specializes in providing IT operations and engineering services to large Danish financial institutions, including Jyske Bank, Nykredit, Bankdata, BEC, and SDC. Growing both organically and through acquisition, the company provides financial solutions to 15 Danish banks.

IBM DB2 for z/OS is a key enabling technology for JN Data, with around 100 DB2 data sharing members hosting development and production services for its customers.

JN Data recognizes the importance of staying abreast of the latest developments within critical infrastructure components such as DB2 so that it can continue to deliver the best service to its clients. The company was a prominent member of the DB2 10 Early Support Program (ESP) and was keen to repeat the experience when the DB2 11 ESP was announced.

Operational Enhancements

According to Systems Programmer Frank Petersen, the operational enhancements within DB2 11 for z/OS have the most immediate business value: "Items such as the ability to interrupt persistent threads can be used almost immediately and will make a big impact on us in the short term.

"I expect this will allow us to use some BIND parameters that should give some significant CPU savings—especially for highly used packages driven through persistent threads, which are used widely in our online systems."

Addressing Challenges

"Equally, the move to 10-byte LRSN/RBA log addresses will be important for us. We hit the RBA issue on one of our DB2 systems a while ago and had to take manual action to resolve it. We're expecting to encounter the same challenge again within the next couple of years, so it's great to see a properly engineered solution from IBM. DB2 11 gives us total flexibility on the path of expanding the RBAs and LRSNs, showing that IBM understands the challenges customers are facing concerning availability."

Petersen adds, "DB2 has been on a journey for many years to provide customers with 24-by-7 data availability. DB2 11 brings the ability to do more object changes online and to rebind packages in use, which will lift restrictions that currently present challenges for sites like ours."

Easing the Operational Strain

Like their counterparts in many other organizations, JN Data's technical support staff never seem to have enough hours in the day.

"We love autonomics. DB2 11 has some really nice features for reducing the burden on the DBA, such as the automatic cleanup of pseudo-deleted index entries," says Petersen.

Online Upgrades

Sticking with the operational theme, Frank Petersen is also impressed with the improvements in the DB2 11 upgrade process, which make online upgrades more feasible. During ESP testing, JN Data used the IBM Optim™ Query Capture Replay (OQCR) product to capture workload on a real production system, then replayed that workload while attempting to upgrade one of their test systems to DB2 11.